MDP

Management Development Program

by
Mark A.J. Dickinson

Dedicated to:
Limo and Alexander
My dear friends Kenneth & Sunchai
Jorge & Eddy

CONTENTS

1. Welcome
2. So Now I Am A Manager
3. The Art of Thinking
4. Change You Before You Change Anything
5. Influence
6. The Other Side of Leadership
7. Hospitality Relativity
8. Master Salesman's Toolbox
9. Sit and Watch
10. The Final Whistle
11. Motivation and Delegation
12. Evaluations Revisited
13. Interviews
14. The Way We Talk
15. The Details are in the Sugar
16. Thank you

1 WELCOME

So here you are! Welcome. As you read these words I want you to remember one thing: the fact that you are reading this book means that this book works.

There are literally millions of books out there that are shouting for attention. Famous people are telling you to read the book that they just read; our friends and colleagues tell us to read a certain book or another, but here's what I have figured out: People are telling you to read this or that, do this or that, go here or there because they did We love to live within the realms of what we have learned or experienced, and then advocate it to those we know and love.

With this in mind, I want to recommend this book to you.

Why?

Because I have lived and experienced everything that is written here and I have practiced it. I have had an amazing life to date. Been broke several times. Times with not a penny, and times of travelling First Class and stretch limousines. I've been a director in the number one hotel in the world, shaken hands with some incredible people like Nelson Mandela, Margaret Thatcher, served Her Majesty the Queen of Thailand, and yet on the other hand I have reached out to help children living on the burning garbage dumps of Manila, and fed children orphaned in villages in Uganda.

What a wonderful journey. Speaking English, Thai, Arabic, some Japanese and French I understood that the true value of a person is best discovered through their culture, and their culture is revealed through their language.

This book draws on over 30 years of hospitality experience and training. I want to give thanks to the many mentors and influencers who have played a role in my life. Big ones are my Dad (GCD), Tony Robbins, and Les Brown, my brothers John and Chris, my wife and son. The best one is no longer around, oh, I wish that she could read this book, just to say that it's done! That would be my Mom.

I know that if you read each chapter, you will find some cool stuff to help you in your daily activities and I would be most grateful if you would share what you learned with me.

Enjoy!

Ps… if you find spelling mistakes and grammatical errors, they are not that important to me. I just want you to get my ideas in your head, which I am sure you can.

2 SO NOW I AM A MANAGER!

No matter how it happened, we can all remember the first time we got the title manager. For me the whole management thing happened long before it happened.

I was 14 at the time and my sister Elizabeth worked as the Housekeeper of a hotel. She was particularly good at what she did and she was awarded the Housekeeper of the Year by her company in a large and lavish event in London. I went to London with my mother to observe Elizabeth winning her award and heard the speech of the iconic Charles Forte. His speech resonates as though it were yesterday that he spoke. He said, "We are in the service industry. People complain about unsocial hours. But I say, if someone wants to socialize, then that is a social hour, and we will serve them."

This statement alone may have been one of my important formational principles. I have always believed in giving or doing whatever it takes to serve customers and make them happy. I watched Elizabeth receive her trophy and decided that I wanted to be an hotelier.

I had the joy of working in her hotel collecting linen from the rooms and taking it to the laundry. The super thing about this hotel is that the rooms were arranged around a hollow atrium and I figured out that rather than putting the laundry in a basket and taking it down in an elevator, it would be far more economical in terms of effort to just heave it over the side, run down the stairs and collect it. The sound of linen whooshing through the air and landing on the floor with a thud was very satisfying and to my young mind I had found a job that was not only work, but that was fun!

I went on to work as a cook in a cafeteria for employees in a supermarket at the age of 16 and helped to pay my own bills through college. Now college was another story. I wanted to be a chef, but the college in my home town of Doncaster had just started a management course, and the powers that be determined that I was more suited for this new management thing rather than the kitchens. Hospitality Management was a fledgling career and did not have much of the glamour that it has today. Against my will, I went along with it, but soon found that this was what I wanted to do.

I finished my diploma at the age of 18 and got a job that started one week after graduation. If I would have understood what I know now, I may have taken a bit longer to get started with work, but hey, hindsight is easy. I applied for five jobs and was offered two. The one I got into was a tough entry where 600 people applied, and 30 were interviewed. At the end of the interviews 12 were selected to stay overnight at the hotel for a second interview the next day. And out of those 6 were chosen, and I was one of them.

So at the tender age of 18 and 2 months, I left home to find my way. I was a Trainee Manager in a program with the De Vere Hotels in England, and I was proud.

I worked 16 to 18 hours a day six days a week and got paid just forty pounds a week. Not a lot! We worked at breakfast, we worked in accounting, we worked at lunch, we worked in the cellars, we worked at dinner, we partied, we slept a bit and then we did it all over again. It was fantastic. It would have been somewhere around that time that Gleneagles Hotel in Scotland was awarded 5 red stars and pictures were published of the entire team of the hotel standing in front of this castle-like hotel, and I dreamed that one day I would work there.

At 19 years of age and 10 months I was offered the opportunity to become an Assistant Manager in a four star hotel on the south coast of England, and great was my joy. I was now a manager.

I did not know what a manager did, other than work very hard. At that age every person I was managing was older than me. I worked hard again. And played hard. There were days of crisis, both business and personal, but somehow at each step there was someone there to help me through. Richard Baker, Drayson Kohli and Brian Crook were great influencers and (though the term did not really exist yet) mentors.

I thought that being a manager gave me a lot of personal rights within work. I learned to eat well and began to educate myself in food and beverage and I would taste whatever food and drink I could lay my hands on. I went to training courses on how to train, I attended the famous Train the Trainer 1 and Train the Trainer 2, little knowing the effect that these courses would have on my later life.

I grew and moved to another hotel within the group. But I didn't like it. I met my first negative clique there, a group of superior individuals who set out to make life miserable for outsiders. I didn't like it and I searched for a way out.

Dreams will be answered. I promise you!

I found myself in short time on an overnight train to Scotland for an interview at the great Gleneagles Hotel. It was a two day interview and I was the only candidate. I don't remember how much I was to be paid, all I remember is the excitement of the opportunity. And so at the tender age of 21 and 11 months, I became the Back of House Manager at the Gleneagles Hotel, Scotland. Not only that, I had my own room within the hallowed halls of the hotel.

I worked hard. My job was to clean every back area and keep it clean. I did it. I did it very well and I was promoted to the position of Junior Assistant Food & Beverage Manager. I can assure you that was one of the greatest honors of my life. I reflected back upon the pictures that had inspired my desire and understood that real dreams do come true.

I thought, "If I can be a manager in the number one hotel in Scotland, what about the number one hotel in the world?" It became my new dream.

Having served two years in Gleneagles I received an opportunity to go and work in Shanghai at the 1000 room Hua Ting Sheraton. I flew to Hong Kong just before my 24th birthday to become the Senior Banquet Manager at this hotel. I studied Chinese and absorbed everything I could. We worked hard. We would serve 1000 breakfasts before 9am, several hundred lunches and Chinese 11 course menus for 1200 people for dinner. Imagine just how many plates we used in one event! But China was not to be my destiny. Tiananmen Square and the demonstrators put a very quick end to my stay in China and I found myself on vacation in England with no job. Undeterred I bought myself a ticket to Brussels and went to the head office of Sheraton for Europe, Africa and the Middle East and presented myself there to a very kind man who was the head of HR. We clicked and he offered me a job in Nigeria, which I accepted. A few days before I was supposed to go I got another call and was asked if I could go to Uganda. Not knowing much about it of course I immediately said yes and within a short while I was on my way to Africa.

I was Assistant Food & Beverage Manager to a wonderful fellow called Ian Walker. He was laid back and so nice. We worked hard and when I wasn't working hard I was on safari. I met lions when I was on a motorbike and I had a trusty old Land Rover. I enjoyed adventure and there was plenty. I met all of the African Presidents because I was in charge of the banquets where they came for the African Congress Meetings. Muammar Gaddafi was one of our guests!

At some point Ian resigned and was replaced by a fellow that I didn't like, and so I began to look to the future and was delighted to discover that there was a job in Kancharaburi in Thailand. No one knew where it was, and Google didn't exist back then, so you had to find an atlas and have a look. It seemed exciting and I signed up. When I arrived in Thailand our hotel was not yet opened, and I was left to work in an office without any air conditioning in the tropical heat. The sweat would roll down my nose and drip onto my pages. I loved it.

The construction of the hotel was delayed and the quality of the construction was not what Sheraton was looking for, so due to the delay they requested that I would go to Bangkok and work at the Royal Orchid Sheraton Hotel and Towers and stand in for the Director of Food and Beverage Operations, who was going out of the hotel for a month for advanced training. I loved it. I worked incredibly hard. Six days a week and every hour from waking until sleeping.

I was approaching my 27th birthday when I was elected to take over from the previous Director of Food and Beverage Operations. This was a grand moment in my life. We had ten restaurants, banqueting for 800 or so, 450 employees in food and beverage and back in 1991 we had an F&B turnover of $10 M per year. I was a king and I loved it.

In 1992 and 1993 we won the awards as the number one city resort hotel in the world from Conde Nast. I had made it. I was at the top. It was the most dynamic and exciting experience life to date and I loved it. I burned with passion, excitement and enthusiasm and did whatever it took.

Somewhere along the way I got a new idea of going to live in Japan, and sure enough, not that much time later I moved to Tokyo, where I found work at the Tokyo American Club. Not speaking Japanese and not having a residency is a big deal in Japan, but at the Club I found neither to be an obstacle and was hired, initially as an assistant and later as the Director of Food and Beverage. I was wealthy and successful and had begun to really develop my own management style. I did that for almost three years.

One day I took a vacation to see some friends and ended up for ten days in Beirut, Lebanon. That vacation became 21 years, as I moved to Lebanon and made it home.

I consulted, I worked in F&B, I had a company, and I went broke. I worked for someone. I opened restaurants. I did training. I opened more restaurants. I did more training. I got married. I ran away from hospitality to the running industry and worked for the Beirut Marathon Association for five years, only to discover that it was also all about event management and hospitality. I had a son. I returned to hospitality to start my own business and created a TV Show in Arabic for entrepreneurs. It ran for two seasons. Then Mom passed away and I lost my focus. I went broke and really hurt inside. I became CEO for a restaurant company in Kuwait. After 14 months it didn't work out. Lots of internal politics and infighting left me cold. I moved to Thailand to help sell a company. I found that every company has the same problems. They all need structure. They all need good managers. They all need training.

Done! was born.

October 2015 I decided, with the help of my dear friends Kenneth and Sunchai, to make a new company. One that focused on managers and growing managers. I gathered up everything I had learned from all the places that I learned it along the way, and put it here in this book.

I hope you enjoy reading it.

The only thing I would say about becoming a manager is this:

1. Commit to learning
2. Keep your feet on the ground
3. The sooner you learn a daily ritual the more valuable you will be to yourself and others
4. Respect the little guys and make their lives special. Know their names
5. Do what you said you would do.
6. Do it when you said you would do it
7. Know that Love is powerful, especially when you are a manager.

3 THE ART OF THINKING

The power of being a great manager is having the ability to think. Sadly we are all so busy doing our jobs that we don't have the time to think. Because we don't take the time to think we don't come up with better solutions, so we do what is the most obvious. Because the most obvious answer generally works, the effort of seeking a better answer gets neglected, and a slow fog of mediocrity forms a veil over the eyes of management and a sluggish bureaucracy creeps in. Dullness becomes the norm.

Here is a remedy for the disease.

Apple CEO Steve Jobs famously said "the people who are crazy enough to think they can change the world are the ones that do".

Sometimes I imagine a world where everyone is thinking. What a difference there would be. If everyone was consciously thinking, there would be no more war. Money would cease to have any relevance. Passports would disappear. The world would become one place for everyone. Not a sort of communism, but a community of people that respected one another on every level. It's all dreamy stuff. To be practical we have to get it down to a reality that we can use in everyday life. No point in living in cuckoo land.

Do you think?

Thinking requires change, otherwise we fall into patterns that protect our lives, but don't allow us to live to our full potential. Change sounds so easy, but the truth is, it isn't. We can know just by reading a few lines that we need to change, here's the proof of that: List three things that you want to see change in your life. Go ahead and write them here:

1. _____

2. _____

3. _____

Now let me ask you, how long have you wanted to change those things? Sure you have wanted to change at least one of them for more than a while. And that is why we need help to think. Einstein, or Henry Ford or Tony Robbins said, "If you do what you always did, you get what you always got". And that is a powerful truth. Repeating things over and over and expecting a different result is the definition of insanity.

The best way to make the change is to stimulate your brain with something new. You have somewhere between 40,000 and 80,000 thoughts a day, depending on who you ask, the problem is that 80% of your thoughts are exactly the same as the day before. You have to break the spell. You have to increase the number of new thoughts, and create a way to keep on getting new thoughts.

To get you started I want you to **WRITE YOURSELF A LETTER.** Now you are probably like everyone that reads a book like this, and you read the words, acknowledge them intellectually, like yes, write myself a letter, but like everyone else, you think that writing the letter does not apply to you personally. It applies to some other person that is reading the book who really needs help. Not you! Actually this is directed at you, and not someone else. If you do this exercise you will be grateful. I promise you! The power of writing this letter is beyond your imagination.

Write it and I will remind you later as to why you wrote it.

Here's what you need to write. Write to yourself as though 12 weeks have passed, and that you have taken these 12 weeks to work through the 12 different thoughts that we outline in this book. That you have applied some of the things that you have learned and that you are now a different person. Write down why you are now different and what has changed. It is so exciting to get this letter back later on. If you want you can mail it to me and I will mail it back to you after 12 weeks from receiving it.

MY LETTER TO ME: (Who I will be...)

Dear _____

If you don't write yourself a letter (even if you just turn to the back of this book and scrawl something there in the back pages, that counts), then you will have lost the whole point of reading the book, because you are obviously not the person to whom I am writing. So, please don't waste your time going any further. Hand the book over to someone else whom you think needs some help and let them get on with it.

Here's what I want to do now. I want to help you create a new thought in your mind. Wherever you are sitting right now you can do this exercise. What you will need to do is read this, then put the book down and do some stuff. When you have done it, then pick up the book again and continue reading. Here's the stuff you need to do:
  a. Touch a surface near you and feel its texture. Is it cold? Hot? Rough? Smooth? Feel the sensation with your senses. Rub the page of this book for example.
  b. Take in a deep breath. One that pushes your tummy out as you breathe in.
  c. Tear out the last page of this book and crush it into a ball (I reserved a page for you to use for this exercise)
  d. Smell the paper and think what it reminds you of.
  e. Now flick the ball of paper with your hand, or throw it like a basketball.
  f. You are a star in a World Cup finals and you are the one called upon to score the winning goal. Take the paper and get ready to score the goal. Everyone is cheering and chanting your name. You can do it! You shoot the ball of paper and you score. The crowd goes wild. You are the hero!

How do you feel right now? Probably flushed with an elevated heartbeat. And that was the idea. If you have access to something to eat, now would be a good time to have a bite.

Think of your favorite song. Now tap your fingers on your knees in time to the music. Keep on tapping until you really feel the song growing louder in your head. And if you can play the song while you are tapping, all the better. Whatever you do now, make sure that you tap.

As you tap, feel the sensation in your fingers. Feel the music. Enjoy it.

Next I want you to do this old exercise. It's a good one, you may have seen it before. But it is still a good one. Connect all the dots with four contiguous straight lines without lifting your pen off the page.

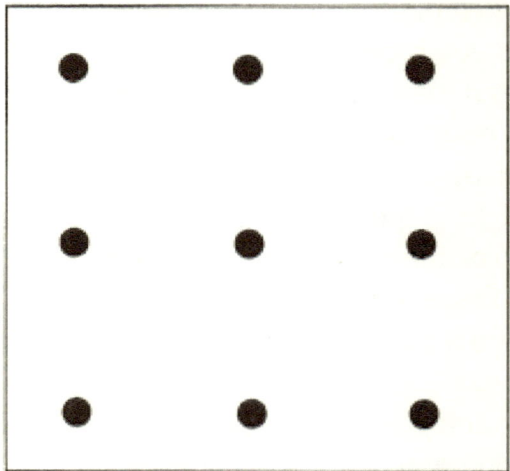

It takes a bit of thought. Of course, if you get stuck then ask my friend Mr. Google to help you with a solution. If you have worked through all of the little exercises that I have just given you, then you will have activated all the areas of your brain. And if you can do more of the deep breaths, then do them. Typically we do all of this in a training environment with lots of music and fun. Sitting alone reading, even if you are on a plane, you can still get yourself where you need to be.

Brain? Switched on. Time to think!

What color is this?

Red, right? Wrong!

It is a mixture of many colors. RGB says it is made up of Red, Green and Blue. CMYK says it is made up of Cyan, Magenta, Yellow and Black.

What is this a picture of?

A dot? No! This is a micro dot picture of this:

DO THIS OR DIE.

Find the relevant truth. Believe in yourself. Stay up all night. Live every day as if it's your first day. Scare your client. Find inspiration everywhere. Stand for something. Keep learning. Get shit done. Don't say yes if you mean no. Treat people as friends not as customers. Trust your gut. Adapt fast. Don't respect the status quo. Define the problem correctly. Break the rules. Put a dent in the universe. Never, ever give up. Don't confuse technology with an idea. Make people care. Risk everything all the time. Tear away the unrelated. Hire better people than yourself. Create influence not likes or views. Don't look at digital as media. Be a master of persuasion. Sell products not yourself. Kick ass. Don't ask research to get an idea. Bring the dead facts to life. Have fun. Be passionate. Don't sell your soul. Enjoy the pain. Don't do ads that look like ads. Find the gap. Ask the right questions. Purify your mind. Walk the talk. Imagine. Inspire. Influence. DOYLE DANE BERNBACH.

So I played with your mind. Why?

I want you to be creative. To be Godlike. Creativity is in your soul. The ability to think comes out of your spirit.

So now have a brand new thought, and don't continue until you have a new thought.

If you have created a thought then you actually created something out of nothing. Before your thought existed there was nothing there. There was no thought. But as you started to think, you began to create something in your mind that heretofore never existed. How exciting is that? And as you thought about it more and more, so you made the thought become real. As it became real it took form and became an existing thing. **Thoughts create things.**

First, you think it. Then it becomes.

Take your phone for example. A long time ago a phone was just a phone. You couldn't carry it around with you. All you could do was go to your phone and make a call to someone else who had to be situated in close proximity to another phone. Today, your phone does everything. It is a camera, a video recording device, a collection of thousands of small useful devices that make you quite the scout. Prepared for everything.

How come your phone can do all of that? Because someone once thought, "Hey, what if my phone and camera could be combined? How cool would that be?" and set about making it happen. You see at first, it was just a thought. But the thought became a thing. The same with your thoughts. First they are a thought. Then they become a thing.

You become the creator of things that never existed.

Why not give it a go? Think of your favorite sport or hobby. Now think about you doing your hobby or sport. Think about the things that are missing from your sport that you wish were there to make it better. What would they be? What do you need for your sport that does not exist right now?

By thinking about this you will have an original thought. You could use random words to help you get thinking. It is a tool of the great Edward de Bono: lateral thinking. Stir your mind with a random word and try to relate your idea through the random word. If you want to find random words, just ask Google. Supposing the random word is "nightmare" and you were thinking about working out at the gym, you could then start relating the words together and firing off ideas. When you run out of ideas, try another random word, like "tulip" and start the process again. Wonderful results start to appear.

Now I think you are ready for our assignment. This session is all about three steps.
Flow
Click
Think
FLOW
Flow is what we have been doing. Getting your mind all fired up and ready to go. Now that your brain is active and you are breaking out into new thoughts, it is time to click.

CLICK
Click is an activation of your mind. A sort of mental anchor point that you use to say, "I am done stirring up my brain, now I need to make it do something useful". So you click. You can click with your tongue and make a sound. You can

click with your fingers, you can tap three times on the table. You can make any sound that you like. But you must create a sharp switch from the dreamy phase to the thinking phase.

Archimedes was sitting in the bath and had his Eureka moment.
Newton was under the apple tree.
Pasteur discovered his rotten bread held the answer to penicillin
Edison had his unlimited trials until he got the one way that really worked

Each of them switched from the constant flow of ideas and attempts at ways to do things when they came upon a workable solution. One that could do the job. And from there on they focused on improving the solution that they were inspired by.

THINK
To think requires unlimited choices, lots of "What if?" questions. A question that I love is, "How can you grow your business by 30% in 60 days?" Man, this question drives everyone crazy. I usually start with a smaller question, "How can you grow your business 7% in three months?" and mostly I am met with massive resistance. The reason people resist is because the number is only a little bigger than what they are currently doing, and you can see the cogs turning in their heads. It goes something like this: "If I am working this hard to get the results I am getting, I am going to have to do an insane amount of work if I am to grow by 7%". As soon as you replace the 7% with 30% (or more), then it radically shifts the whole thinking process and

suddenly people start coming up with brilliant ideas of how to grow by more than 30%. Try it and see what happens: "How can you grow your business by 30% in the next 90 days?"

Unlimited thinking is amazing. It costs nothing other than the few minutes indulgence you give it. Kids do it all the time. The pool thermometer in our garden pool became a golden treasure that had to be protected from the sea monsters at all costs. Actually it is just a pool thermometer, but for an hour or so it became the world's most prized possession and we fought long and hard for it. Lots of water was splashed and many shouts were heard, until finally the sea monster (my son) triumphed and claimed the gold.

We asked an executive team at a company how they would grow their business by 30% and we ended up with a blueprint for a new factory costing a few million dollars being drawn on the whiteboard. Amazing. We didn't spend a single dollar, but boy, did we have fun creating the boundless possibilities available if you just try to think differently.

Be outrageous.
Whatever you do, please don't make silly excuses. You CAN do this. Everyone can do this. You have it in you. Some people say, "I am not good with my creative brain". That is just not true. Yes, of course some people are more creative than others, and some are more practically minded than others. According to plenty of studies your left and right brain fire together and are interconnected. Leftbrain rightbrain is just a myth.

https://www.theepochtimes.com/right-brain-and-left-brain-myth-debunked_246480.html?photo=1

At 22 TB per minute your brain is gathering a massive 372 GB of data every second. That's 1.3 petabytes per hour, equal to 2000 years of non-stop play of 4mb songs, or 48000 miles of 4mb pictures printed out and added end to end. Whatever, it's a massive amount of data being captured every single second.

You CAN definitely use this brain of yours to come up with some fantastic solutions, but the damper on all of this is that your brain processes about 2mb per second!

FLOW is all about getting this brain of yours to start moving. Shift you from your comfort zone.
CLICK is about identifying the moment that you take one of your ideas and begin to mould it into a workable solution
THINK is where you ask yourself outrageous questions that challenge your thinking, leading you to (a) better solution(s).

Take the time now to write down a list of all the challenges that you are facing… get your flow going, figure out multiple solutions and then think.

Challenges	Solutions
1	
2	
3	

4. CHANGE YOU BEFORE YOU CHANGE ANYTHING

The journey to becoming a great manager is learning that the first person to challenge when anything does not go according to plan, is you! No blame, no accusations, just answer this simple question, "I am responsible. How could I do it better or differently?"

A lot of the time we like to blame others because it's the easy option. The power of management is to take personal responsibility. What do I need to do better?

Invariably this question will bring us to a point of self-evaluation, hopefully resulting in identifying an area where we need to improve. That improvement will require change.

If you want to be effective in changing, then for the duration of this chapter I suggest that you turn off your mobile phone, and put it out of sight. Get every digital distraction out of the way so that you can really concentrate on what you need to do. If you do that, you will most likely listen to these ideas, act and change. If you do not, it means that you will hear these ideas, your ego gets in the way, and nothing happens. So just like the previous chapter with the letter, if you won't separate yourself from the phone, then this book is most likely not for you.

If you really want to grow and change in a living way, a way that will resonate through every area of your life, and powerfully and positively affect others, then I highly recommend this formula for you.

First understand that the mechanics of change are really simple. You see a problem, there is a proven solution; apply it and you get the result. Simple. For example, you are overweight. You go online. Get a diet. Follow the diet. Lose weight. Solved. Simple.

No!

There's nothing wrong with the process, but the solution does not work. Why not? Because we are complicated creatures. We understand that to lose weight we must consistently burn more fuel than we consume. Eventually, through wise eating and slightly under fueling our bodies, we will attain weight loss, and of course, we know that if we increase our exercise at the same time, we will become fitter and stronger. Very easy.

Still NO!

Our heads get in the way. Our old selves, the fat one, gets in the way. While logic and reason suggest the path to a better life, there are old habits and emotions that block the way. Over and over we lose out to our old selves. Change is not to be found in the logic, but in our beliefs and values; the things that we think about, what we listen to and what we do with our time determine if we will change.
The beginning of change is that we must first understand and accept that our life is controlled by our own decisions. Each interaction in your life comprises decisions, and the ones you elect to make will determine your life.

Ultimately, "You Control Your Life".

You live your own movie. You are the scriptwriter, director, hero and producer. Whatever your movie is like, is of your own construct.

Is it a horror movie? You made it so. Is it an adventure movie? A blockbuster thriller? Whatever it is, you made it so.

Is your life boring? You made it so.

In order to change there must be a full acceptance of your personal responsibility. The time you turned left not right, the time you said yes not no, the time you slept in when you should have woken up. Each decision led you to where you are right now.

This very moment, the one in which you are reading this book, and these very words, is like the spout of a pot. Everything inside has led you to this tiny aperture where you will squeeze through to an entirely different and new reality.

The point is this. Not whether you are in control of your life, nor whether you agree with me or not, but rather, if you FEEL like you control your life; and that is far more important.

I find that the more people that I talk with, like the audiences that attend a training seminar, the more I see a common thread. By our logic, we know that we are in control, but by our lives we live as though we are not.

There is a very simple reason why this is the case, and it is this: to change is difficult. Others around us will challenge us when we start to change. We may be teased or even ridiculed.

I was fat, incredibly fat. 131kg. When I went on a diet the number of people that offered me cake, candy and sweet things was insane. When I told them, "No, thank you", they tried hard to give me something sweet. They called themselves my friends. Why did they offer me sweets? Because if I lose weight and become fit, they will be challenged by my example. So better than facing a new Mark, one who is fit and healthy, and who would then challenge them on areas of their own lives, they try to hold you where you are.

Same for working out. Same for quitting smoking. I stopped cigars, I used to smoke three a day. When I stopped, my friends would justify how only one would not do me any harm and actually encouraged me to compromise my decision. I lost a few friends. But I quit smoking!

It's easy to figure out what you need to change. You don't need me or anyone else to tell you where you need to start. Just ask your conscience. It will speak up real fast.

THINGS I NEED TO CHANGE NOW:
1
2
3
4
5

See, there you go, now you have a list. How long did it take? 20 seconds?

You know what you need to change, now let me ask you this, can you find the best way to get it done? Most probably yes. Diet? Getting fit? Finding a partner? New job? You can find 123,159,652 answers on Google search. Easy. You are ready to change.

Sadly that is only 20% of the job done.

80% of change is in the mind. You need to activate your brain so that it desires that change, otherwise your desire for change is going to fall flat on its face.

In order to increase your chance of success there are some things that you are going to want to do to secure this success

MY FAMOUS FIVE - MESPF
My Famous Five are the backbone to my change: MESPF. Mental, Emotional, Spiritual, Physical and Financial. These five areas of my life must all pull together to get me where I want to be. To do this, I like to create for myself a circle of people that help me focus on the five areas of my life. Instead of just rushing to write down a few things on a list, I want you to create a lasting path to your better self.

Successful change will come when you create a solid plan, and *execute* that plan. Let's look at the five areas of your life, Mental, Emotional, Spiritual, Physical and Financial (MESPF). What you need to do is to think carefully about five individuals that you know and admire who are strong in one of each of these five areas of life. Think of a different person for each one of the five areas. The key here is that the people you think of must be stronger and better than you in that area of life and you must respect them for what they know; once you have selected your five people you are going to enlist their support in helping you to grow. People who are better than you are going to be able to help you to acquire a higher level of skill, knowledge or experience in that area.

So now, if we are to figure out how to really change, we look at our list and categorize the change we want to see happen, allocating our change list into either Mental, Emotional, Spiritual, Physical or Financial, and then putting the names of your five people into one of the five areas too. If all of this seems a little overwhelming, then to get you started right now, you may select just one thing in one area of your life and work on that, and as you grow in your first area, you will begin to figure out the other people that you want to have as your Famous Five. If you are thinking, one person can do all of this for you and meet your needs in all five areas, it may be true, but here's the thing, if you go to only one person then you are going to burden them with a whole lot of your problems, and they are not going to stick around for long. If however, you divide up your life into five areas, then you are going to be sharing a part of your growth needs with various different people, and only one part of your challenges shared with one person is going to be a light load for that one person to help you with. Remember, if the person you have chosen is strong in one area of your needs, they will be very happy to help you out and encourage your growth. What I have found to be true is that as you share your challenges with your Famous Five, not only are you growing, they are also benefiting from you too, and so it becomes a two way process.

Once you have identified your five people, you are now ready. Set up an informal coffee, a walk, a meeting or similar and then get with that person and talk to them about what you want to change. That person being stronger and better than you are in the area that you want to grow, will help you go after it. It will be a natural process.

"Hey, Anthony, I've been thinking about losing weight and I am not succeeding in my diet plan. What did you do to get fit?" And away they go. If you listen, even take notes, by the time they have finished talking you have all the info that you need from someone whom you trust about how they did what you are trying to do. "Anthony, I need to ask you a favor. Can you check up on me a week from now and see how I am doing?" and guess what? They will!

There's no need to get all technical with your selected Famous Five and start revealing your plan, at least not to start with. Just keep it to yourself and get on with growing. Your Famous Five don't need to be informed that they are one of your wise counsellors.

The important thing about all of this is that you have to go out and do what you have decided to do. This is where most people fail. Getting your friend to help you is a good way of making yourself accountable for change, and lets them feel that they are a part of your success. As you keep on spending time with your Famous Five, so you will share with them what they have helped you to achieve, and how they are a part of your personal growth team. It's wonderful.

Your Famous Five will be delighted to help the more you are grateful. They may even set out on their own MESPF journey.

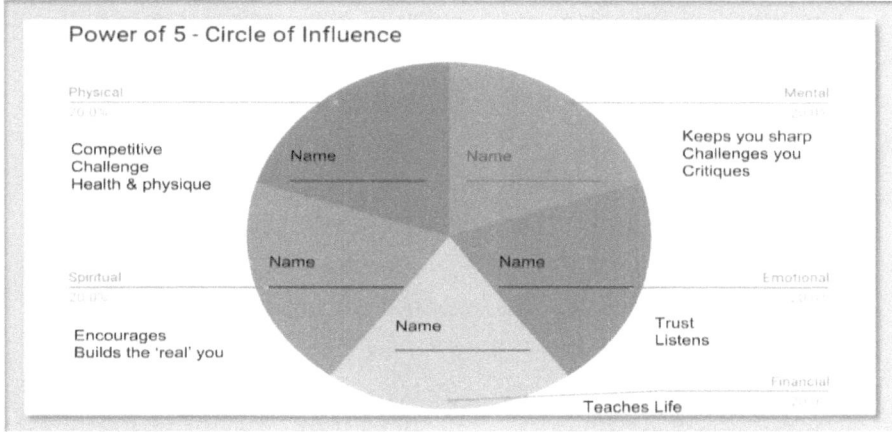

To make our changes stick, we need to get our brain to do its magic. It needs to endorse our decision with some chemicals. Dopamine, Oxytocin, Serotonin and Endorphins all have a great role to play here. If you think back to 25th December just past, I am sure you can remember where you were and what you were doing. However, if I ask you to tell me what you did two Tuesday's ago, you probably wouldn't have a clue. What's the big deal? Chemicals! Your brain gave you a big dose of good stuff when you were celebrating with your loved ones. It was so strong that it stuck with you. We need to do the same to get you through from where you are to where you want to be.

The power of this game, as I have learned from Anthony Robbins and others, is three key things.
1. Focus
2. Get Help
3. Resolve Inner Conflicts

FOCUS

Simple to say, just a single word.

The world is pulling you in every direction that they want you to go. The news, advertising, your friends, social media. It's a full on war for control of your mind. You have got to focus.

The best way I have found to focus is my first 20 minutes every day. Wake up. Find a place to sit where you can see natural daylight. Take out a sheet of paper and write the word "Thankful" at the top of it.

Then write down every single thing that you are thankful for. Once you have done that, then write down 3 simple things that you want to accomplish in your day.

Have 3 major goals that you are working on, that have a long term delivery date. Say 6 months to a year away, and re-write those every single day.

Make a list of your personal commitments to yourself, like getting into the best shape of your life, or running a distance in a certain time, or whatever it may be, but write it down.

Do it all on one piece of paper and then keep that paper with you throughout the day.

This is focus.

By doing this every day you will see a pattern start to emerge in your life. You will begin to see that there are consistent themes in your notes and you will begin to experience growth towards your goals and you will see the successes starting to pile up.

You will be pleasantly surprised as happiness starts to grow on you. You will feel more giving, more loving, more serving and more in tune with your soul. Actually, by focusing daily on being grateful you will automatically begin to change.

You will extract from your notes the things that you truly want to change by re-examining your goals each day, by writing little daily goals, by keeping up with your promises to yourself. After a while you will know exactly where you are heading and what you want to accomplish.

I remind you that the very fact that you are reading these words is the proof that this process works. For this book was once just a few words written down as a goal on a piece of paper. And now? Here it is. So it works!

Focus on a few very important things - not a long list
Understand where you really are on these things right now
Decide where you really want to go with your goal

You see, if you do this in the morning when you wake up, and you actually write it down with a big pen on a big sheet of paper, there is something in this process that engages you and makes you feel good. By saying thank you for everything you can think of you open up your mind at the beginning of your day to powerful and positive thoughts.

You will naturally feel good. And then as you write out your three daily goals you will feel a sense of life and passion creeping into what you write. Finally, writing down your big goals every day makes them live in your mind. It makes them real and clear and your imagination begins to mix in with your writing and you begin to create your dreams as you live your daily life.

Recently we bought a telescope for my son, Alexander. We set it up in the garden and I got the moon positioned perfectly in the viewfinder. I called Alexander to look, and in his excitement he grabbed a hold of the telescope and looked through the lens, but all he could see was a black sky.

"Daddy, I can't see the moon!' he wailed.

I could tell him that the moon was gone now and he would never be able to see it. I could belittle him for grabbing the telescope. I could tease him.

Or I could encourage him. Help him find the moon and experience his squeal of delight as he saw the breathtaking magnificence of the full moon in all its radiance.

We are like this in our lives. The goal was to see the moon through the telescope. Never having done it before, Alexander had no prior knowledge of how wonderful it could be. He just had an idea that he had heard it might be fantastic.

The telescope was there, the lights were off, and it was a full moon. Everything he needed to accomplish the task was there. The only problem was a very tiny adjustment was required.

How often we give up right when we are about to succeed.

Wherever you are right now, I want you to do something very bizarre. I want you to take in a deep breath and push your shoulders all the way back. No matter where you are, just do it. Push your chest out as you breathe in, and then look around you and say, "I am doing it!"

"I am making the change I need".

"I am doing it right now".

"I own this".

"This is my focus!"

And right now, you are most likely smiling.
If you can't say it out loud, still get the shoulders back, breathe deep and imagine yourself saying these words.

You have already began to change.

RIGHT HELP
Moving the ball down the field is a task. It is not easy. One man or woman can rarely do anything of major consequence all by themselves. You will probably be able to give me some examples of a few who did, but if you really look you will find that there are many people behind the great success stories in life.

A coach is paid to get an athlete to deliver his or her best. A consultant is paid to help a business grow and deliver its maximum potential

To be outstanding, we need help.

Ego tends to get in the way and we think that we can do it all alone. The problem with this approach is that the more we progress the more blind we become. We reach the point of having considerable knowledge, but that very knowledge becomes the barrier to our growth. Our ego says, I know a lot about this, or I know all about this, what can someone else teach me? And so you buy into your own lie and settle for average.

When I want to grow, the first thing I do is I look for the best people who are already doing what it is I want to be good at. I analyze them, I examine them, and today we are blessed with YouTube and Google and so on, who freely and willingly provide us with an abundance of information on virtually any topic on earth.

So I look for the person who does what I want to do, and who does it really well.

Then I do what they do.

Some may say that this is called copying. I say it is smart. You begin with copying, but as you learn the lessons, so they become your own. The stories become yours. The lesson becomes yours. You become the lesson.

Wonderful. You learn by watching great people. You emulate them. You become one of them.

Help is a fantastic resource. The fastest path to learning. Learn without the pain of making their mistakes, make your own mistakes, but at least you can shortcut some of the pain.

We wrote our MESPF partners down already earlier on in this chapter. What I want you to do now is to think about five global leaders that you could aspire to be, one in each area:

Mental	_____
Emotional	_____
Spiritual	_____
Physical	_____
Financial	_____

Put a name of someone next to each one. Someone that you could aspire to be. And now go find out all about them, how they got where they are, and start doing similar things to what they did, and in effect, you are getting them to help you.

I wanted to grow my presentation skills. I wanted to be more effective on stage. I wanted to teach powerful lessons. I looked around the world and found a fellow called Tony Robbins. I went and signed up for his event. 60 hours later I came away with a new life perspective.
I have a friend who challenges me think about the way I do business - Nadim
I have a coach, full time in my life - Jorge
I have spiritual friends who encourages me to have spiritual thoughts - John & Georgio
I have a friend who challenges me to be physically my best - Anthony

And I have a friend who helps me to be financially solid - Roland

Five people all helping me to grow. The great thing about these five friends is that they are all better than me in the area of life that I share with them. When I feel I have learned what I needed to learn in one area, or I feel that I am at a plateau, I search for a replacement and seek to grow in new things.

The process of getting help drives me to drop my ego and to become a student. To learn as much as I can so that I can grow stronger, better, more powerful, more loving, more giving, more serving: MORE!

I would like to remind you of one important point, what is so cool about this process of getting help is this; you never burden just one person with all of your life. You have five different folks around you all helping you to grow. Some of them you only ever get to talk to by voice contact (Skype etc.), others face to face. Get these five folks onto your roster and start the conversations. By time you will figure out if you have chosen five that can help you, or if you need to switch them around.

It took me two years to find my first five, and from there on, it has been an incredible journey.

INNER CONFLICTS
If there is anything that will mess you up when you are on your way to change, it is an inner conflict.
I mean, you are set, you have taken your decisions, and you are ready to go. And you begin, but come the first day

of your diet you find yourself invited for dinner, so rather than mess up the dinner by being a spoilsport, you think to yourself I will leave it for tomorrow, and start then. But tomorrow never comes!

It's the morning. Today you are going to start your day with 20 minutes of focus. You hit snooze, just 5 more minutes of sleep and I will be ready. Suddenly you are late, never mind, tomorrow I will do it. But tomorrow never comes!

You decide to work out for ten minutes, but when it is time to get started the phone is blinking. You decide to answer the message, but there is a cool link to a video. You follow the link down the time drain, and suddenly it is time to go to work. Tomorrow. But tomorrow never comes!

Busy worrying about what other people think.

That's what holds you back.
Eat healthy. Let everyone else eat whatever they want.
Let people laugh at you. They will not laugh when you are benching 100kg
Write your daily focus. Your intensity will shine like the sun.
Leave the phone for later. After all, it has silent mode and missed call mode for a reason

DO NOT LIVE FOR WHAT OTHERS THINK OF YOU.

It will kill you.

Forget what others think of you.

When Mother Teresa was 39 she first began working with the poor on the streets of Calcutta; there was no one watching her.

When Nelson Mandela was slogging it out for 27 years in prison, no one imagined that this prisoner would become president.

When the Austrian soldier snook out of the barracks and jumped a train to a bodybuilding contest, little were they to know that Arnold would become a movie star or a governor, or Mr. Universe.

None of these amazing humans were focused on what others thought of them, they did whatever it took to live out their beliefs and to follow their dreams.

The Bible says, "Love your neighbor as yourself"

Many have called this the golden rule, and I am sure that everyone that reflects on these words agrees that it is a great way to live; but it begins with a very important principle, the love for yourself, first. How can you give love if you have no love?

How can you give and serve if you are running on empty. How can you give advice if you have not yet lived it yourself?

Borrowed words sound hollow and everyone knows it. Love yourself first. Get up there in front of the mirror every single day and tell yourself that you love yourself. Yep. Look yourself in the eyes, full on, and say it: "I love you".

Do it every day and you will be different. What will be different? Try it and see. Seriously. What happens is that you think about loving yourself, so you begin to take care of yourself in small ways. Like when you fall in love with someone, you do stuff for them that you would never imagine yourself doing, so it is with loving yourself. You begin to take care of yourself in better ways and that reflects on the outside. You become a nicer person, a better version of you.

As you love yourself you will feel a sense of peace and calm in your life. Your mind will present to your consciousness areas of your life where you need to resolve issues. You will remind yourself of places where you need to go and make amends.
Get it done.

That is solving inner conflicts.

If you do not solve them, you will be in a constant battle with yourself and you cannot grow. Change will be hollow and you will be dragged back down.

Stop fighting you.

You deserve to be successful and you deserve to be wealthy, whatever wealth may mean to you, and you deserve to be happy.

You see, this part of the process is something that you are going to have to work hard on. Your ego is going to have to take a step backwards and you are going to have to man up and get on with some fixing.

There will be some tears. But you can do it!

Go solve the things that you know need to be solved. You know exactly what they are. You may not want to tell anyone. You may not want to voice them out. But you know what you need to fix right here and right now.

So go do it. Get it out of the way so as you can move on. It's critical.

When I was looking to get married, I could not find anyone to marry. I tried and I tried. I looked at every girl I met as though she may be the one. I had a list of criteria that she had to meet. I actually don't think any woman could fulfill my list. One day, a wonderful thing happened to me. I reached a point where I just decided that I did not actually want to get married at all, and that I enjoyed the freedom of the single life and I was truly very fine living out the rest of life as a bachelor. I bought myself a Porsche, a lovely single room apartment on the seaside overlooking the Mediterranean and a round the world Business Class ticket.

I began to live a single life with gusto. I was no longer looking at women as potential partners, just as friends. I had more fun. I was free. And then suddenly I was married! How come? I dropped my ego, I stopped fighting. I met Rim and now we have been married for a long time.

If you are a gossip, like to gather round to hear the latest, you listen to the news and read the newspapers, you are stuffed. You have no hope! You have bought into the theory of golden captivity. Mediocrity. The life where there is no real pain, no real emotion and no sense of victory. Don't.

Be a leader. Stand Tall. Be different.

When you align yourself with goodness and you focus on what you really want, you get the right help and you remove conflicts, your life accelerates faster than ever before.

Achievement will follow.

CELEBRATE
And once you achieve, then it is time to pay it forward. Celebrate your success, it is important to enjoy the moment of success. Make sure that you put real effort into rewarding yourself for what you have accomplished. For each change you make, give yourself a special reward. One that will have deep meaning to you personally, that will be fun and help you to enjoy the beauty of your change.

Make sure that your celebration is contained. Confined to a specific moment or activity, and that you then return to the great lifestyle that you have created that has allowed you to reach your success. There is great temptation in celebration, the temptation to overdo it or to prolong it, and then suddenly it is no longer a reward, and it has become the new norm. Be careful.

After celebration you are now charged with an important responsibility: Pay it forward to someone else. Give them from what you have achieved. Make a meaningful contribution to someone else's life.

Change is a core element of leadership, for when you lead others you will naturally call them to change. The lower your ego the more you change; the more you change the more you will affect others, the more inspirational your story will be and the more lives you will influence.

Change: This is true success.

5. INFLUENCE – A SECRET!

This chapter is more like a conversation between me and you, so let's just imagine sitting together in two comfortable armchairs facing each other. Got it? Great. So let's begin:

One of the most powerful tools I have come across is the subtle art of influence. Now some people are really uncomfortable with this idea, they consider it manipulation. One time I taught this course about influence to a group of managers that I was working with very closely, and for several weeks afterwards, one of the group would not talk to me anymore. He was convinced that I had been manipulating him. Recently we were having a conversation again, and he had changed sides. He is now a true believer and uses these techniques in his daily work. So, manipulation, influence? Both are effective. What counts are the motives behind why you use these techniques. If you are giving, loving, serving and focused on building up others, then it is going to be called influence. If you are mean, self-focused, ego driven, then it is going to be called manipulation. So take a moment to figure out which side of the fence you are on.

Here we go. Influence is all about getting what you want out of a situation. A great video to watch on YouTube is Derren Brown influencing Simon Pegg on selecting a gift, or Derren Brown influencing a girl to buy a giraffe named Frank, using influence, or as he calls it, perception without awareness. Both are funny videos, but both put over a very important point. We are all susceptible to being influenced without really realizing it.

As a manager in business today, one of your most powerful tools can be using influence. I consider this chapter a kind of secret. The reason it is a secret is that in order to be able to work your magic, the audience should not know the mechanics of the trick. If you know how to pull a rabbit out of a hat, don't tell anyone. Surprise them and then move on. As my Dad used to say, never do the same trick twice in front of the same audience. It's the same with using influence.

Keep it a secret.

INFLUENCER VS. INFLUENCEE – KNOW WHICH ONE YOU ARE

In each encounter, particularly in business, you must always know which position you are going to adopt for the interaction ahead. Typically, the person that requests a meeting is going to seek to influence the person they have asked to come to the meeting. For example, if you ask for a sales meeting with a prospect, you are going to try and influence them to buy your product. It's the same in a communication meeting. You ask for a meeting because you want to achieve something. Either you want to get your point across, you want agreement on an issue, or you want to learn something. In all cases, one will be the influencer and one will be the influencee.

INFLUENCE GOES TO THE ONE WHO IS BEST PREPARED

Knowing that you want to influence someone during a meeting provides you with the will to prepare in the right way for the exchange ahead. It will give you power and confidence as you plan for your meeting. To be able to influence, you must know what you want. Decide what it is that you want; exactly. Take time to write down your desired outcome. Next, you picture the outcome. Visualize it. This is really important and takes mental preparation.

Think about the meeting. Picture the room in your mind. Figure out where the participants are going to sit, and figure out where you are going to sit. Think about what you are going to wear and how you are going to dress, and have an idea about what the other people in the room are going to be wearing too. As you seek to gain influence, it will start from preparing the smallest details. Play it out in your mind. If you don't know the room where you are going to be meeting, then try to get there a few minutes earlier, the day before if you can, and check it out, make up some reason, such as you have a presentation to give. This will allow you to get a clear mental picture so that you can visualize the process. If you are there beforehand you can ask, "Where does the person you want to influence normally sit?" Perhaps it is a meeting room where you are the boss, and you want to influence your group, then take command of the room and don't let anyone mess with your arrangement. Put your stuff on the place where you are going to sit before others get there. If you have never met the person that you are trying to influence, search social media to get a face in mind. Check out their profile picture, it says a thousand things about them. Get a feel for what makes them tick. These are the weapons of the influencer.

All this preparation is unseen by those whom you wish to influence. Now that you have prepared everything in your mind, play the meeting through. Figure out exactly what you want out of this meeting. Know your outcome precisely.

Know your minimum outcome too. Imagine yourself getting the deal at the highest outcome. Play it in your mind. See yourself shaking hands with the person that you have just influenced, you have a big smile on your face, so do they. They are agreeing to what you wanted. Imagine it. Picture it. Feel it. Breathe deeply. Get that successful feeling.

There is no fear. You know your minimum outcome and you must not settle for less. Ever.

Remember, you must be willing to be flexible in the light of reason. You would also do well to remember that you can withdraw to think again, and you do not have to settle right here and right now. If someone is pushing you to settle right here and now, then do not settle. We will talk a bit more about that in a moment.

Accepting a different outcome and being willing to think of different outcomes may be to your advantage, it may turn out better than how you had expected. Being prepared to think carefully at the time of the meeting will help you to lower your ego and open yourself to better alternatives. Emotion and being emotional will slow things down.

Influence is dissolved by words such as ME and I.

Influence is multiplied by words such as YOU, US, And OURS

In your preparation you should take the time to weigh the options that you have. Write them down. Basically, you want to get something that someone else has access to

and can provide you with. They can provide you with several things:
- Approval for something
- Give you something
- Connect you to a resource that will give you one of the other two

In all cases, the person you are seeking to influence is the gatekeeper. You need them to open the gate.

STUDY THE SITUATION
Think about the person, or people that you are going to approach. As we said, if they are an unknown, then do research. If they are known to you, then run through the different ways you have seen them react and respond to situations in the past. Try to remember a situation where you have seen this person agreeing to something similar to what you are looking for, and find out how it 'went down'. What was the conversation like? Who was there? What did they ask for? How did they ask? What did they get?

Emotional states of your influencee are really important. It is extremely hard to influence people that are in an angry state or distracted state, unless you are seeking to incite them to rebellion or demonstration, in which case the more anger and emotion the better. In our day to day work we are most likely trying to find positive outcomes; avoid angry. If you face negativity you can take full control of the meeting by doing a stretching exercise or a breathing exercise. I do those a lot with senior executives. There is a part of every person that loves to do the unusual. If you cannot get through the tenseness and create a new ambience, perhaps the best idea is to propose to postpone the meeting and suggest to meet another time. These two tactics can turn the mood in the room. When you instigate an exercise or activity you are taking control of the room and developing massive influence, particularly if you get everyone to stretch or breathe in time with you. In this case you are now unquestionably in control of the room and your influence has gone sky high.

KNOWING WHAT YOU WANT IS RARE

A lot of people *do not* have a crystal clear vision of what it is they want. They are insufficiently passionate about what it is they are doing, so any outcome is ok. They appear before the person they are seeking to influence with insufficient will and desire, so much so that they cave in long before they get what they want. Knowing exactly what you want means thinking it through and writing it down in advance of your meeting. The result of 'caving in' breeds resentment and discontent and causes anxiety that leads to anger and frustration. People walk away and disengage. Who is to blame? The person who did not prepare.

You want to exert influence? Know **exactly** what you want. I repeat this point, know **exactly** what you want. Write it down. Not an agenda. Not a meeting idea. Not the presentation you are going to give, but a <u>written decision about exactly what you want</u>. Be as detailed as you can be. The outcome will startle you. The more precise you are, the more focused you are, the more you increase the odds of getting exactly what you want. The thing is that you can repeat this outcome over and over again, by being prepared and knowing exactly what it is that you want.

PLAN A AND PLAN B

Part of gaining influence is to carefully set a trap. This is very intelligent. What you want to be doing here is sharing your problem without yet revealing your solution. A lot of management books teach you to show up and state the problem and the solution. I am not a fan. I think when you show up with your hands open and looking for help it displays a lot of maturity. Not only that, others will reach out to support and help. This is highly advantageous as you may be presented with a much better solution than the one you originally had in mind. How we set this up is what is important. The preamble is rather like creating the scene at the beginning of a movie, or a fine novel. Here is the garden, everything is green. It's really rather beautiful. However, it seems we have a problem with cats coming into our garden and I am not really sure what to do about it. I have some ideas but wanted to know what you think.

The average human being will fall for the trap every time and will begin to share their "wisdom". Very few will throw the ball back at you and say, "What is your solution?" The ego driven age we live in is somewhat of an advantage as people will quickly shift to being the hero in the garden. They will suggest their solutions.
You as the influencer keep quiet. Listen. Take notes and play the humble student. If you hear a solution that is better than yours, jump on it, add your thoughts, you are a double winner. If there is no solution equal to the one that you have, but one that may have elements of what you want, then you pick up on that, and build on the solution that is appearing in front of you as you talk.

Lead with lines such as, "That's a great idea. We could add this and that to it too", and now you have a done deal. You have buy in.

Single bullet. Plan A is adopted and approved and away you go.

Alternatively, no one has any idea and they don't like your Plan A, then go for Plan B. Plan B is a collection of thoughts on a theme. You propose a bunch of ideas or a basket of solutions that can get you closer to where you want to go. Here you talk about other gardens where cats no longer walk, and devices that have been installed for preventing cats from climbing on the walls, and bait traps for catching the cats and taking them to adoption centers, or taming the cats and making the garden a cat friendly place. As you talk you see which way the story is moving. Finally what is important is to have consensus over having cats, or not having cats in the garden.

TIMING YOUR ARRIVAL IS CRITICAL
Being late can be good. If you are the influencer with authority in the situation, being late gives more authority and an air of importance will fall over the situation and enhance your influence. A tension will be created through the awkwardness of your late coming. This plays into your hand if you are seeking to dominate a situation. It is not a card I advocate.

Being late can be very bad. Arriving late when you are the influencer with no authority in the situation will disadvantage you like nothing else. You want to be there five minutes early at least, and not more than 9 minutes. If you arrive too early you are sending off a signal, but by arriving a few minutes before time you provide yourself with a clear advantage of being able to prepare yourself and do the things we talked about in regards to setting up the room.

Starting a meeting with an apology for anything is relinquishing your influence for no gain. Avoid it.

START BY SMILING

Winning influence is done by smiling. When you smile, others will smile. You will relax tension and create warmth. If you smile and everyone else is serious, your positivity and power will make the change. Stay positive. Stay smiling. It is eventually irresistible. Like telling someone not to laugh at a funny movie, the harder they try not to, the more they will laugh. Your smile states confidence and control. My smile says, "I am calm and I am in control". Have this thought before you enter the room and it will resonate through your words. Actually you may not be calm at all, but the very act of smiling will help you appear so. It is critical to walk into the room with confidence, shoulders back and head up when you are seeking to make a decision that requires people to place their confidence in you. Prepare by taking deep breaths before you enter the room and push your shoulders back and stand tall. Be nice!

GET PHYSICAL

Make sure that you connect physically. If the layout of the room is difficult, walk around to the person that you are going to negotiate with or with whom you are seeking to influence. Give them a firm handshake with 5% more strength than the hand shake they give you. If you are in the Middle East and you are going to kiss, do it with firmness and confidence. Hug if you can. Hugs build influence. Make it strong and short - more on that in a moment.

Always try to be on the right hand side of the person with whom you are shaking hands, That way, you are reaching across your body. The person who is on the left hand side has to do an awkward sort of twist around to shake your hand and they are disadvantaged. Power comes from being on the right. If you are on the left, then turn towards the person to shake their hand face to face, even if it is a photo situation. Shake hands then stand side by side for the photo!

When I want to control or exert influence I use touch. There are many ways to do this. We have already talked about the handshake. Another way of increasing influence in the handshake is touch the elbow of the other person while you are shaking their hand. This increases your power.

You may face a dominant hand. This is one where the person you are shaking hands with has their palm slightly facing downwards. This is very dominant. Do not react other than as you shake their hand, correct the angle to be equal and 90 degrees to the floor.

You may increase intimacy and influence by shaking hands with your left hand on the shoulder of the person that you are shaking hands with. This is a power builder and demonstrates control right from the beginning.

As I mentioned, sometimes I just blast through it all and give a hug. I push the hand aside and say, "Hey, give me a hug". That throws people off track big time and creates an incredible bond. At other times, I will get everyone in the room to hug each other once the proceedings have started, and I will target to hug the person that I am seeking to influence during that process. Obviously people will feel uncomfortable at first, but if you build it into what you are doing, it will work well, and you will reduce tensions, creating closeness in the room. After all, it is influence that you seek, so use incredible tools to get outstanding results.

Another kind of handshake is to cover the hand of the other person while you are shaking hands. This is a control signal too. What you do is you shake hands in the normal way, then take your left hand and put it on top of the shaking hands. Do it with a big smile and while making eye contact, and in a friendly way you will generate another subtle signal that you are in control. Influence grows.

If you receive a masonic handshake, ignore it, even if you are a mason. If you don't know what one is, it is not important, for those who do, keep that level of influence aside. I am not one.

One of my biggest power influences in touch is to lean on a person. It is insanely powerful. You get in close proximity and actually lean on the person. This is a massive power shifter. You need to practice this a lot. What you actually do is when there is a point of complexity that requires explanation, you take a paper and marker pen out and draw a simple solution. You then actually get up and go near to the person you are seeking to influence and put the paper in front of them and show them what you mean. As they look down so you put one hand on their shoulder and say,

"See this?" and point with your free hand at the paper. They will look where you are pointing, that is human nature, but the connection will have been made.

If you are close to the person you are seeking to influence you may also use touch on the forearm. Tap their forearm while you are talking and point to something else. Connection.

Cementing influence can also be achieved by the use of post influence decision hugs. This is where you have obtained the decision that is closest to what you had desired, and you go out there and give a bear hug of gratitude. Make sure that you gauge it right and don't end up overturning the decision. The key to the post decision hug is to be genuine.

BEWARE THE POWER THIEF!
If you walk in with all the confidence in the world, others may try to steal your high position. They will say things such as, "You look good, but you look like you gained some weight" or "wow, are you ok? You look a bit stressed". You must not fall for this trick. It is a one-upmanship game where the other person is trying to counter your confidence and poise. What they are subtly trying to do is to take control. Your reply to this situation determines whether you maintain the upper hand or lose it. Just simply reply, warmly and directly, "Really? Not at all" and smile. "Perhaps it was just a thought crossing my mind". You keep your influence! Water off a duck's back is the appropriate analogy here. Whatever you do, do not react. It is a rabbit hole. Don't go down it or you will have lost your influence right there. The

rest of the meeting will be a formality and all your planning will be lost.

Frowns, downward shoulders, dragging feet kill influence.

There is one entirely different scenario, where you will do the opposite of everything that I have just said, and that is when you are really 'down and out' and at the last straw and you are seeking help. Then you want to have a small smile, shoulders slightly curved, no frivolity, and a handshake that is not more than equal to the others. A slight sadness of expression, and a thin smile will win the day.

MIRRORING

Much has been written about this, but the important thing is to do it. When you want to obtain influence through mirroring you start by carefully and approximately doing what the person you are trying to influence is doing. So they may be leaning back, gradually lean back. The key here is not to be overzealous. Do it slowly and carefully, as though it is subconscious. In practical terms most mirroring is done subconsciously. What you are seeking to do here is to mirror the person you are trying to influence, which is to put yourself under their influence, and then at a certain point you will then lead with a change in posture. Supposing you were leaning back, then you will lean forward and put your head forward, and hands up on the table. If the person you are seeking to influence starts to follow your lead, then you are now in control, you have switched power from them to you. If they do not move, and they remain in their leaning back posture (or whatever position they were in), then you slowly unwind the position you have taken until you are almost neutral. Then you await a shift in posture from the person you seek to influence and mirror again. Your goal is once you are mirrored, you will then take the lead. If you get the lead, you win the deal. Smiling and nodding is a great way to start the mirroring. If you smile and nod enough, most people will end up doing the same, especially if you ask a question to which the answer will be "yes". Once they mirror you, you have more influence.

SHIFTING POSITIONS
During the process of getting what you want, you can shift positions several times. You can start off by being the influencer, shift to influencee and back again. If you give the impression that the other person is in control of the situation, and that you are under their control, you can advance your cause quickly. Listen, smile, nod your head and agree a lot. Just by listening well, and jotting notes while the person you are seeking to influence is talking, you are preparing to shift position. People love to feel that someone is listening to them, and by taking notes, they will feel a sense of importance and growing authority. You are giving them respect and control. This is being a fake influencee. You must remember that this is only a phase in the process and that you are going to reach a point where you are going to take control. When you are up against powerful egos, this is a magical tool. Let them feel that they are in control until you are ready to state your case.

DO NOT LOCK IN A DEAL YOU ARE UNSURE OF
When you have created your clearly desired outcome in your mind (and on paper), and established the minimum that you are going to settle for, then you must keep to your commitment to yourself. If a deal is on the table that does

not suit you and about which you are unsure, do not lock it in. Once you agree it is really hard to reverse. Decisions are still fluid until you say "yes". As soon as the big word crosses your lips, the deal is done. Negotiation from there onwards is all inconsequential.

IF YOU DO NOT AGREE, THEN DO NOT AGREE.
Most people mess up right here. We have all done it and lived to regret it. What I have learned about agreeing and saying "Yes", is this. When we are so focused on a decision, or we are working through a situation, we become massively connected to it emotionally. A deal being offered that is close to what we wanted, or meets many of our minimum criteria will often seem tempting. The thing I have learned, painfully, is this. **Reject it.**

Anytime it does not meet your minimum requirement, reject it.

I will say it one more time. Reject it. Yes. That's right. Reject it.

Bad deals are bad deals and they always fail. If you make a bad deal for you, you will resent it later and you will cause the downfall of your own decision. If you agree to do a job, but the money is too little, you will not work on it with all your heart. Ask me, I know! It will be a burden and not a blessing. Bad deals eventually always fail.

If it is a bad deal for the other party, they know it and one day they will break it.

We have all heard of win-win.

WIN - WIN - WIN
But I believe there is a better way, it is win-win-win. There are usually more parties to a deal than just the two at the table. Crafting a win-win deal for the two parties at the table is fine, but what about the final beneficiaries of the deal? Will they win too? IF the answer is yes, and it is a win-win-win, then it is a great deal. Sign it. Shake on it. It will win!

FAST FOLLOW UP – FIRST TO FOLLOW UP
Influence is not just about what happens in the meeting. It is what happens immediately after the meeting. By being the first to follow up after the meeting you will maintain your influence and may craft the deal in your favor. Because you are the first to frame the meeting response, you can do it by saying, "here's what I understood and here's what we are planning to do". If you have improved things a little since the meeting, you can mention that, and say so, and providing you are reasonable you will most likely gain approval. Major shifts will not work.

If you are late to respond, you will be at the risk of being given the deal from the other person's perspective, and they may craft the deal missing some of the issues or details that are important to you.

Being late also means that you will have to apologize for being late, and this means that you cede your influence to others for no reason. Rather like being late to a meeting.

HERE'S WHAT I UNDESTOOD
This is a great sentence for starting your email. It makes allowance for others to continue the dialog, but states

clearly what you want. Certainly it must be on the terms of what was discussed, but it will be in the language and a frame of your choosing.

WRITE IT
A handshake is easily forgotten. The words that were said in sincerity will be quickly lost in the fog of our fast paced lives. People are so distracted and bombarded with an excess of information that they will quickly drift into other things and you and the decisions that were made will drift too. Whenever it is written down we create a fixed point of reference. If people say that a handshake is enough, remember that it is not enough. Write it anyway and send it over with a preface saying, "I know we are all good to go on this, but I just wanted to reconfirm what we have agreed." If you think you will need it later on, then make it legal from the beginning. A few bucks spent to legalize a document is worth way more than years of resentment after a deal has gone bad. Anyone that will not agree to a written agreement is not serious, and therefore you do not have a deal.

INFLUENCE CAN BE GROWN – FIRST PLANT A SEED
When you plant a seed, you are preparing for influence in the future. What you do is put an idea in someone's head for a time further down the road. This can be very subtle. In general people hate to know a little bit about something but not be privy to the whole idea. A powerful seed that you can plant goes like this, "I would like to talk to you about an idea; do you think we could meet sometime next week?" A typical response will be to question you on the idea immediately. Avoid it. Say, I am still working on some details, but I think you are going to like it. Smile too! You will

make people crazy with curiosity. The subtle approach. You will get your meeting!

Another way of being subtle is to start speaking and then stop mid-sentence. The listener will want to know what comes next. But you politely decline. Say you want to think about it before you share it and that you shouldn't talk about this. And don't say anything more. Again, their curiosity will give you influence. The other party wants to hear exactly what you have to say. And now! Don't give in.

Planting a seed takes careful thought and preparation. So when you have decided what it is that you really want, and the outcome you want, then create a plan for the seed that you want to plant, and go for it.

EMOTIONAL APPROACH – YOU GET ONE CHANCE
Earlier on I alluded to this, if you come into the meetings with a thin smile and shoulders down you are going to be able to leverage influence. You are appealing to pity and compassion. You are calling upon people's sympathy. This will work, but it is a bomb. It is massive.

YOU ONLY GET TO USE THIS ONCE!

If ever you decide to go for the emotional appeal, make sure that you have thought it out very carefully. You burn bridges with this approach that you cannot go back over. Basically as you use the emotional approach you are using all of your influence to get a very specific result; help of an exact kind.

Normally it works if you project sincerity, genuine need and pain. The objective here is not to be a sniveling or complaining object of sympathy, rather a strong person who has been cracked by a situation that is just too big to carry and you need help.

Reach out, be personable, show need, but demonstrate there is still control. Show examples of efforts that you have made but that have not succeeded, and that you are still capable of making decisions, but not this one. You will get the help you need.

Tears are a last resort. They are extremely powerful. If you believe that they are the tipping point, and the help you need is important enough, then go for it, again, do not overdo it. A tear or two, not a flood! Demonstrates inner strength and humility and the urgency of the need.

In this case, allow people to reach out to help. The worst thing to do is having generated influence, meaning people are reaching out to help, then pushing them away. You MUST allow them to reach out and support you, otherwise, they will think you rude and ignorant. Kindly accept support, an offered tissue or a glass of water is well received with thanks and a small smile.

The influence is complete and the deal is done.

You get this once!

If you do it again you are a basket case and no one can or will help you. Cry wolf.

KILLING THEM WITH KINDNESS
My Mum used to say there are more ways of killing the cat than stuffing it with cream. I like to think that an overdose of kindness creates massive influence. Most people do not hear kind words in their daily life. The majority are disgruntled and have an axe to grind. Something does not please them or is not up to their liking and most of their time is spent dealing with problems. Then along comes this bright person, you, full of kindness and nice words.

You reach out to them with genuine feelings. You compliment them, or their business, or their office, or some other detail that you are aware of. Not only doing this once, but giving intelligent praise throughout your meeting. Great idea. Hmmm, I wish I would have thought of that. That's smart. And similar. You light them up. Tell them you like their watch, or how they are dressed. Rare are those who give praise and compliments. You give them, be genuine and you are going to be loved.

What you are doing is providing your listener a dose of serotonin. The happy drug. Their brain begins to respond and sends out a good feeling. Ask for what you want. Big smile and ask...

INTELLECUTAL APPROACH
Here you are going for the person who has an ego based upon achievement. They have created an aura around themselves of knowing. They know. They know what they know, and they also think that that means they know about many things. The style here is compliments. Compliments to someone with a high ego softens the ego and opens the

doors. Listen a lot. Let them tell you what they know, even if they don't know.

This is difficult to do because all along, your own ego is going to be tapping at your head, saying, "Noooooooooooooooooo" and you are going to be thinking lots of negative thoughts. Practice praising people all the time, so that when you get into this situation you can do it naturally.

You have to remain focused to use this approach. You cannot skip a beat. If your attention wanders off somewhere you will lose your influence. Stay razor sharp. Listen and make grunting noises appropriate to the flow of what is being said. Avoid interruptions and take notes if necessary. Allow and encourage your target to talk more. The more you do this, the more you will become in control. They will begin to feel that they are doing all the talking, in the end they will run out of steam.

At this point you will ask your first question, which is actually the key to revealing the problem, so for example you will say, "What would you suggest I do about the cats in the garden then?" and you pitch them your problem.

This person will then share with you a whole list of ways that they have overcome that or similar problems, and from their great wealth of knowledge (aka ego) they will be 80% of the way to solving the problem for you, perhaps even engaging themselves in the solution.

When you are ready, you will then engage this person as a free resource for helping you solve your problem. You have created a personal advisor and for free!

BUT I AM THE BOSS
When you are the boss, and you have the influence as a hierarchical right, then you have the influence. Someone once famously said, "Speak softly and carry a big stick" What you should be aware of in this case is that you will often be on the other side of influence. You will be the influencee.

Watch out!

You have read some of the strategies for influencing others, so be ready for these strategies to be deployed against you. Try to sift through the control being used against you in your lofty position and consciously fight to put your ego aside as much as you can. Avoid falling into the baiting trap.

When asked for advice, be ready to counter, "No idea, what are you thinking?"
Remember, NEVER have all the answers. Tell people to, "Ask Google".

Your role in maintaining influence is to ensure that you get people to think for themselves and to become better individuals in the process. The more they create their own solutions, the greater you will be.

If you are driven by the sense of always having to be right, then you are probably more often wrong, but your ego blinds you and you feel just fine. No one ever tells you that you are wrong? A sure sign that you are on the wrong path.

SOMETIMES THERE IS NO TIME TO DEBATE. I AM IN CHARGE!

There is a situation that needs immediate decision making, so take the decision, which is the power of influence. There is an emergency, just get everyone focused on doing a task that is helpful towards the goal of solving the crises. As people get engaged in solving it, slowly step back and give up control to others. This is a direct approach. You are in charge for just as long as you need to be, and then you offer up influence to whoever shows up that is capable of taking over.

THE FIRE DEPARTMENT USUALLY USES WATER TO PUT OUT A FIRE

Shouting never got us anywhere. Why people still do it, I don't know. The louder you raise your voice, the less influence you actually have. If you are a screamer, it will work for a limited space of time, and then it will wear off. You will create fear, and out of fear comes stupidity. People then no longer think for themselves, they wait for you to step forward and take all the decisions. And as soon as anything goes wrong, they are excited to help shovel the blame onto your shoulders. Angry people shouting destroy themselves and their influence. It is only a matter of time.

What's funny is, people can hear much better what I am saying when I say it quietly!

I AM SORRY. PLEASE FORGIVE ME

These six words are amazing for rebalancing influence. When you are wrong, get on with it and own it. Perhaps it does not work for politicians, though I rather think that most people would prefer it if they would say sorry.

In work it is a charm. You disarm the other person. Now here's a thing, I have come across people that have felt entitled. There are quite a lot of those around these days, if you use this technique with them, prepare yourself to be met with an even more entitled person. Keep in mind, you are apologizing for you, not for others. You are making peace with your soul.

In general, what I find is that with sincere people or genuine people, when you use this technique you get a wonderful response. You come first to the problem with a genuine and brief apology, get it out of the way, then you will be able to solve anything. You gain influence because of your humility and away you go. And as you may remember from the previous chapter, if you keep unresolved conflicts they will hold you back, which will reduce your influence, but getting things resolved gives you power.

Having a long term goal in mind is valuable. It will help you avoid striking out for a quick gain when actually what you need is people to be on your side for the future. Always try to focus on building influence both for now and the future. Once you have created bonds of influence, you can call on them over and over throughout your life.

SURRENDERING YOUR INFLUENCE

Sometimes you will come into contact with someone that is very capable of influencing others. Be aware and on your guard at all times around these people. Measure the actions that you are taking, be conscious of your mirroring, and answer questions that you are asked with patience and wisdom. If you do not pay careful attention you can end up doing things that later on make no sense whatsoever, and you will wonder why you ever agreed in the first place. Younger people are easier to influence.

If someone starts to compliment you, be aware of the possibility that they are not just being nice, but perhaps trying to influence you.

BEWARE OF GIFTS!

Most gifts come with a price tag on the back. Remember that.

BAD INFLUENCE IS EXERTED BY GREAT INFLUENCERS

Throughout history there have been many people that have had very bad intentions, and they have influenced millions, even entire nations, to follow them blindly. It is important to guard our minds, being aware that we are open to be influenced in our thoughts by the messages that are constantly thrown our way. Erosion of values is through insidious bombardment by multiple micro messages. They come through social media, news channels and finally through public opinion. Whatever is keeping the mass occupied, is created to exert influence. Think about it.

Observe the memes in children's games. The viral messages on different social media channels. The campaigns against ordinary moral values through high profile apparently meaningless media battles.
All of these seek to gain influence over your minds and change the way that you think.

MASTERS AND SLAVES
Influence is so very real and powerful. From a child being offered a drug that tastes like candy to a kid having their first cigarette, they are products of influence. Half a trillion dollars a year are being spent on advertising. Products could just as easily be provided to us in simple unbranded paper bags, but no, we have a world full of choices, where every choice is a battle of wills. Make yourself aware of the influence war for your attention and guard against it.

Finally, if you want influence, one of the best ways to get it is to give people what they want. Not what you want. And that is perhaps the success of every great brand, campaign or belief.

People want
    POWER
    PRESTIGE
    POSITION
    PRIDE

When they are powerful, they think they are in control. You can influence them
When they seek prestige, they can have it by helping you.
When they have position, they can show their position's value by helping you

When they have a lot of pride, their ego will give you what you need

So let others use their power, prestige, positions and pride to help you get what you want, while enabling them to do their thing.

The thing that will kill your influence faster than anything else are the following:
- Over Familiarity - get too close, lose your influence
- Gossip - destroys influence
- Failure to deliver your part - when they commit, you commit and deliver
- Boasting

INFLUENCE IS AN ART. IT TAKES TIME TO MASTER IT
- Know who you want something from.
- Prepare really well
- Select your technique for influence

Go get it!

6. THE OTHER SIDE OF LEADERSHIP (NOT MANAGEMENT)

Napoleon Hill wrote a book called 'Think and Grow Rich'. I suggest you read it.

The problem with books is that once you have read them then you must do something about what you have read. Typically you have two choices, do something, or do nothing. We seem to live in a culture today that says you must read as many books as you can. There's even a bunch of different apps that will consolidate the best of books into a moment's thought so that you can say you have read the book. So okay, you read them, but what do you do with what you have read? The real point of reading a book s to discover something new, to inspire, entertain, educate, encourage real change, or give birth to a new thought or share an idea. It is supposed to propel one forward, transforming the reader to a new and more enlightened state; hopefully better than when they started the book.

Reading a book for the purpose of reading it, is of no value at all.

This chapter is all about leadership. I hope that you will read it and be inspired to do something with what you have read. Whenever I have the chance to talk about leadership I always feel like I am treading on sacred grounds. There are so many who have gone before me who have spoken eloquently and powerfully on the subject, and to be honest, the majority of people that I meet throughout my days are usually well acquainted with a style of leadership that they have found to be comfortable or effective for them.

So here's how I want to kick off this chapter, with a question: What is leadership to you?
Please take a moment to write down your top ten words that define leadership for you:

1	2
3	4
5	6
7	8
9	10

Well done! You are right. That's leadership!

Tanya Prive wrote an article in Forbes about the top 10 qualities that make a great leader. She wrote that having ideas, honesty, ability to delegate, communication, confidence, commitment, positive attitude, creativity, intuition and ability to inspire are the qualities of a leader. You probably included some of those in your list. She had over 7 million views for that article alone.

I was stunned. 7 million people viewed an article to discover what one person had to say about leadership. Is it true? I guess so. Ten paragraphs did it. So what am I going to write here? Nothing. This chapter is done. You got it.

6. THE OTHER SIDE OF LEADERSHIP (NOT MANAGEMENT)

Actually, here we are again. Same chapter, but a restart. "The Other Side of Leadership". Textbooks are great. Books on leadership are abundant. Articles on leadership are helpful, LinkedIn has thousands, HBR has hundreds, and Forbes has loads. YouTube is rich in videos and clips that encourage learning in leadership. Great speeches are inspiring and motivational videos will get you fired up. My latest Google search revealed 621 million results for articles on leadership and 6 billion results for the word Leadership!

But in leadership there is a secret that is not much told.

As with all great secrets, you are not going to get it so easily. You are going to have to work for it. Actually, you are going to have to earn this secret! Here it is:

THOUGHTS ARE THINGS
Seriously. The secret of leadership begins with this, "Thoughts are things". Thoughts are as real as the words on this page. They begin in our heads, they swirl around and suddenly become clear in our minds. When they become clear then we can do something with them. That is why we say, "Thoughts are things".

FUNDAMENTAL: A thought is as real as a car, a phone, a bike, or any other object.

To understand leadership you must understand this: "thoughts are things".

Have a thought!

Just one.

It can be a flash in your mind.

But this thought is the seed of leadership.

Whatever this thought is, you must *desire* it more than life.

You must *grow* this thought.

Intensify this thought and let it become your *defining* purpose.

That is the essence of Napoleon Hill's book.

If you did not yet have a massive "life-thought" for your life, then you are probably not ready for this chapter. A "life-thought" is a defining moment through which you obtain clarity about your life's purpose and for a time it is clear to you what you will do with the rest of your life. Many people never have a "life-thought" because they have never prepared themselves to have one, so when their "life-thought" comes along, it just passes them by.

I want you to prepare yourself for an incredible thought, your life-thought. One that will change everything about you, for now and forever. You never know when your life-thought is going to appear. How do you get yourself ready? You get yourself in the best shape of your life, mentally, emotionally, spiritually and physically. Now this takes effort.

You need to plan and work on getting ready. We talked about this already, MESPF.

Once you are prepared, you are ready for your life-thought. Remain ready, and never stop being ready. Decide: even if it takes the rest of your life, you will remain ready.

Maybe your great life-thought has already come along, you've had it, but perhaps it did not yet convert from a thought into reality. You will know if you have had your life-thought because the one that I am talking about is the one that will become a single powerful driving desire. Most people have not found theirs. It's easy to know who has found their life-thought and who has not.

Those who have, are on fire. You touch them, they burn you. With their passion and their ambitions. They are doing amazing things, things that seem to magically appear for them without effort. Their work is invisible, their results speak loudly. These are they who have found their life-thought and are driven by it.

If you have one brilliant idea, one life-thought, THE ONE that you really believe in, you must fan it into flame. Do everything you can to make it burn brightly.

Note this, when you are not ready your opportunity will not appear. Or worse still, your opportunity may appear, but you will not see it. Opportunity wears many disguises.

I was interviewing candidates for a CEO post during the past few days. I have a war chest of 250,000$ a year to spend on the right person, and more if they are outstanding. People start to talk to me, through the interviews I ask each of them what their vision is and why they are currently doing what they are doing. Imagine, a potential CEO candidate saying that he sees that the market is too difficult and that the competition is too tough. Right there, at the beginning of the interview he disqualified himself. His moment of opportunity was there for the taking, but he messed it up. He blew it. The opportunity came, passed by and left. The candidate was unaware. He was unaware because he was blinded by the immediate challenges in front of him and was not focused on being an outstanding CEO candidate. You see, to get the job of CEO you have first to become the candidate for the position, afterwards, from the position of candidate you stand a much better chance of becoming the CEO. To be the candidate you have to project the readiness to create a better future for an entire organization, no matter the market and the challenges today.

When you don't know what you want, you will not recognize your opportunity even when it comes along. When you are surfing along just looking for anything that might give you money, you will not see the real opportunity. That candidate was too busy projecting his ego rather than trying to be the leader of the company that we were looking for.

If you have received your life-thought it will become the engine for your desire. It grants you the ability to know exactly what you want. It can discern the steps that will grow your idea, and ignore those that will slow your idea. Once you reach this point, you are at the moment that your life-idea will begin to transform from a thought into a thing. Now you know what you want. You must work to define it precisely, clarifying exactly what it is that you want. Writing your thoughts into words, and drawing them so that they begin to live.

Your life-thought is clear: fan the flame of your desire to get what you want.

To get the thing that you want you do not need money, or education or influence (though they are helpful), these are not the key. What you need is a desire so strong that you will do whatever it takes to get what you want.

Most people don't get what they want because they quit.

Napoleon Hill tells a beautiful story called, "Three feet from gold". It is a chapter in his book that you should go and find. Arnold Schwarzenegger shares his story in a powerful video on YouTube that in essence is saying, "Don't let anyone tell you you can't". Both stories are fantastic examples of what you can do when you know what you want.

You must stick at it.

Tenacity, staying focused on your life-thought no matter the obstacles, despite opposing forces and the various naysayers. You must fight, and keep on fighting.

You may fail at the beginning. I failed in three businesses and lost over half a million dollars in the process of getting to this line in this book. So yes, you may fail. It will hurt. It will be hard.

Failure is temporary. You think that you are failing. You think that you are failing because you look around you and you see others doing better than you. You see others who are further ahead than you. What you don't see is the hard times that they went through to get where they are. For every business that is succeeding there are so many that never made it. For every business that is struggling, there are hundreds like it. The measure that you use to decide that you are failing may be wrong. Perhaps you are not failing. You are just under pressure to deliver at a higher level than you ever did before, and because it is not working out first time you are rating that as failure. You need to get external perspective. Just because the money is not there, or perhaps worse still, the debt is there, you feel that you failed.

The amazing thing about these perceived failures is that later on, they will become the story that you tell of how you became a success. The failure is awesome. No matter how hard it seems. It is a part of your success story. You will come back to it and tell how you overcame to reach the top of the mountain.

Success follows failure.

You need only one idea to succeed. As you succeed you succeed beyond your original dreams. Your state of mind changes. You get energized by every little thing around you. You make life changes and you stand tall.

You are definite in your purpose. Determined. Impossible no longer exists.

Where did this start? Knowing what you want.

My question to you today is simple: DO YOU KNOW WHAT YOU WANT?

The key words in this sentence are simple, YOU, KNOW, WHAT and WANT.

Frankly if you are a consumer of many books you are probably about to skip past this step. However, this is the core of the entire book right here:

Get YOUR life-thought of WHAT you WANT.

Once you know what you want, your entire life will be transformed. Very simply. As you think, so your life will become.

Literally, if you want to be in great shape and have an outstanding body, and that is your true desire, you will automatically change the things that you eat, the places that you go, the time that you sleep and all things related. You will become a machine that creates an outstanding body. No one and nothing can tempt you… you just become it. Temptations will abound. They will come from all quarters some that you would never expect. It's not just the desserts or candies that people offer you, no, it is the emotional temptations. If you are intensely focused you must work with all your might to stay focused.

A very dear friend of mine passed away on Monday. He was the person that inspired me to start my company, Done! He picked me up on a bad day and asked me why I was so frustrated and sad. His question was followed by a reminder to think, "Blue Ocean". If you haven't come across this concept then go read the book, or get a summary online! His challenge was basically stop looking at the lack of opportunities and hard challenges, and see the open horizon of opportunities. The day that he passed away I was incredibly sad, but focused on being focused. I determined that nothing would distract me from my goals. But by Friday of the same week I gave in. The inexpressible sadness washed over me and distracted me from my goals. It was a week of gradually slipping down a slope. The workouts went first. Then the discipline of eating, and then I started the oversleeping. All in a week. The outcome? Gaining weight. Sad. Loss of focus.

The temptation did not come in through the front door. It wasn't a piece of sugar that broke me. No, it was the game that our minds play on us. Reliving our friendship in my head brought me to my knees in tears. And yet, the joy of our times together were wonderful and I now lift up my head and say, Kenneth, wherever you are, as ever, you are an inspiration of love and kindness. This book is because of you. Eternally grateful.

When you lose your focus, get back up and go right back to where you left off. Skip the guilt trip. There is no need. You cannot say that you lost time. You just used your time for something else. Something that for a moment was more important. Your soul needed to go there.

A lot of folks have real trouble coming back to where they should be. The thing is, if you come back right away, you will do fine. The longer you leave it the harder it is. If you missed a day, just start right back. Get the ritual going again. Count it as a break. A reward. A rest. A time that you needed. And now you are back.

Focused. Laser Focused!

It is important to remember that nothing happens to you. You are in charge of you.

When your purpose is clear, the universe will answer you. Things will flow to you and not away from you. You become like a magnet. You really do attract the things that you are looking for.

I meet a lot of folks who say that the attraction doesn't work. It's really interesting that if you ask those same people about the economy, the current climate, their personal situation, they often say it is bad. Then you ask them how is business and guess what, they say it is bad.

When people say, "Everything is bad", what do they get? Bad. How do they feel? Bad.
When you watch the news how do you feel? Hopeless.

This thought is easy to go along with. Negativity breeds negativity. Most people agree and say, "Yep. True!"

Why will people agree with the negative so easily, but fail to see that the opposite is perfectly true?

If you dress up real nice every day, stand tall and walk with confidence, speak nicely with people and never complain,

what kind of life are you setting yourself up for? A good one!
Exactly.

Will it make you wealthy on day one? No.

Will it make you wealthy by time? You better believe it will.

You will stand out as an ethical and reliable dependable individual. There are few of those around and you will be in demand.

I don't know what it is that you are looking for out of life, but I am sure it is more likely to be something good rather than something bad. So get focused.

If you are overweight, do something about it.
If you are unemployed, do something about it.

"Oh Mark, you don't understand".

Oh yes I do. I understand that you are so comfortable with your whining and complaining attitude that it scares the heck out of you to get off your comfortable chair and do something about where you are at. I have been there. At 132 kg and comfortable, yes I have been there!

Desiring what you want is not enough. You begin with the desire. But then you have to do something. You need to make a plan.

DESIRE IS YOUR STARTING POINT

I have longed to play the guitar all my life. I watch people playing the guitar and I have the thought, "I wish I could play the guitar". January 2018 I decided that wishing was useless. Wishing I could play was not going to get me anywhere, rather like standing in the garage and wishing I had a Ferrari will not make it happen. I have to do something. So I bought a guitar. I began to play it. Now that we have the wonders of YouTube to help us out on virtually anything, I have master teachers at my fingertips.

Today I can now play some tunes on the guitar.

Where did it begin? Desire. What came next?

ACTION!

The thing is, now the guitar has become a burning obsession. So instead of sitting in front of the TV of an evening, we sit in the salon and talk and play tunes on the guitar.

I no longer hope that one day I will play the guitar. It is not a wish. It is a reality. It is driven by a desire. I began at the age of 53. Now here's how I think about this: I picked up the guitar for the first time at age 53. It takes ten years to become really good at something, so by the time I am 63 I am going to be really good at this guitar thing. That is so cool. That means that hopefully in my older years I am going to be able to sit around with my friends and play some cool tunes while we all have a good time. Campfires and marshmallows here we come!

That is definite purpose.
I practice every day. The guitar is always around. Sometimes in the morning, sometimes in the evening, but every single day I play a bit more. Practice scales, chords, strumming, new tunes, learning to read music. It's all fun.

What about you?

What do you want?

I want to have a PhD in Neuroscience/Neurology. I want to do that by the time I am 77. That's a 25 year plan. So now, I have begun my journey and I am studying the introduction to the brain. It is compelling, fascinating; one of the most unexplored areas of the world. Incredibly interesting.

Yes, I have taken that decision, and I am working towards it.

I think about it like this. I have made my way in life to this point without much of a plan. I just bumped from one thing to another and onwards. What if I have a great plan? Where would I be able to get to? So now I am living out my plan. I love to stand and speak on the stage to audiences about how to manage, how to train and how to grow. I am getting quite good at this now, but imagine that I practice it for another 25 years, and I constantly learn and grow along the way. Where will I be at?

Desire. Burning Desire. Unwavering Desire.
I don't care what the critics say. They tell me I am nuts. They laugh behind my back. It's ok. I am not doing it for them. I am doing it for me. I am doing it for you.

I want to give, love and serve as long as I am alive.

That is my burning desire. I will do it. Till I die.
I feed my desire. So must you.

What's the difference between success and failure? Being 'The One' and just someone?

Burning desire.

Hill's six steps are here for you to read:

1. Decide EXACTLY what you want
2. Decide EXACTLY what you will give to get it
3. A definite date that you will be done
4. Ready or not, create a plan and start immediately
5. Write a clear conscious statement of exactly what you want and when, what you will give to get it, and the plan for how you will do it
6. Read your statement out loud twice a day. Once in the morning and once before you sleep

That's it.

Does it work?

You bet.

You are probably sitting there reading this and going, "That's it?"

Dreams start as a dream, and for a while they are just that: A dream. If you do nothing about it, it will become what is called a daydream.

But if you decide to follow these steps you are going to rock your life.

So what happens next?

Nothing!

OR

Something incredible.

Right here, right now, could be the defining moment of your life. You are an author, a singer, a composer, an artist, a speaker, a talented something or another. What you are is inside of you. Unlock it and set yourself free. Start with Step 1:

1. Here's what I want:

2. Here's why I want it:

3. Here's what I am going to do to get it

4. This is when I want it to be done by

The why is as important as the what. If you are serious about changing an area of your life and moving forward on your dream, then take the time to START.
Perhaps you are bound up in your spiritual beliefs and feel conflicted. Let your 'why' be to glorify your God. That makes it pretty spiritual. Maybe you are worried that your 'what' is to have a bunch of money and someone told you that is wrong. As soon as you figure out your 'why' you will change your outcome. Once you believe in it, it will happen.

THIS IS NOT A MAGIC SPELL. It is only for those who are willing to work hard and grind out *every single day* to get what they believe is theirs. It is for everyone who will create a daily life ethic that is ready to receive ideas and work on them tirelessly until they become reality. And once they become a reality, to keep on working on them until they become a success story.

THE OTHER SIDE OF LEADERSHIP (not management)
This chapter is called the other side of leadership (and is not about management), and that is because I am not here to teach you what others have already mastered. I am here to share with you a simple thought on what real leadership truly is. Here's what it all boils down to:
- Many people read books on life improvement (like this chapter)
- Most of them are too distracted to really focus
- Only a tiny number of people actually read what has been written, hear what has been said
- A smaller number believe what they have read
- An even smaller number of people actually do anything about what they have read

- And an even smaller number of people stick with what they heard, and do it

HOW IS THIS LEADERSHIP?

As soon as you accomplish growth in your own life, and you recognize that you have moved forward, then you automatically share it with someone. You share it because it bubbles out of you. You share it because you are compelled by a mysterious inner force that causes you to tell others about it. There's no one telling you to share it. You just do.
As soon as you share it with someone else you are showing them the way to a better life.

Someone who shows others the way is called a leader.

So rather than trying to figure out what leadership is, and learn lots of cool tricks and tips to be a great manager, rather grow your own life, find your life-thought, dedicate yourself to its pursuit, be passionately consumed by it, and as you grow share it with others.

Leaders are those who have a clear vision of their own life-thought and pursue it all costs until it becomes a reality, or until they find a bigger dream that takes over from the previous one.

Live out your life-thought and you will know the way of leadership without anyone telling you anything. You will craft a way that is your own. You will create your own rules for what a leader is. You will have your ten rules of leadership. Surely you will learn from others things that you can add to your style, but first, get that life-thought clear in your mind and focus on it. Desire it. And never, never give up on it. Your passion for what you do will attract others, they will follow you, and you will be a leader.

7 HOSPITALITY RELATIVITY

$E = MC^2$

Energy and mass are the same physical entity and can be interchanged.

This discovery by Einstein has had an immeasurable impact on our world; from atomic bombs to GPS signals, this equation has transformed our world.

Now I want to transform the hospitality world. The theory of hospitality relativity.

$$P = \frac{C4 + SW + S - E}{L}$$

$$\text{Profit} = \frac{\text{Capital} \times 4 + \text{Smart Work} + \text{Sales} - \text{Expenses}}{\text{Luck}}$$

We can impact every element of our equation. The goal of our business is profit, and since this is an equation we can re-express it like this

$$\frac{\text{Capital} \times 4 + \text{Smart Work} + \text{Sales} - \text{Expenses}}{\text{Luck}} = \text{Profit}$$

What does this mean?

If we have capital and we multiply it, and we work smart, we create sales; take away our expenses then we will have profit. However there is always one unstable or uncontrollable element, and that is luck.

As hospitality professionals our mission is to work on the elements that are within our control, so let us focus on Capital, Smart Work, Sales and Expenses.

Those who are mathematicians are going to have a problem with our formula. Any ideas what that is?

C4
Why is this an error in the formula? Well for example if you invested $3 Million in a project then this formula is going to say that you should have an investment of $12 Million. Obviously we are not advocating putting 4 x your investment into the project, so let's look again at our formula. C4 or Capital x 4 is created to show that there are 4 types of capital, and you can multiply them all. Since we have created this formula, it is ours, and this is the way that we want to write it; for us simple hospitality folks, this formula serves our purpose.

Our four kinds of capital are
    Financial   - the cash tools used to create the business
    Human   - that's me and you - intellectual/knowledge/ideas/experiences
    Social   - reputation/relations/connections/trust
    Material   - physical stuff/infrastructure/plant/premises

FINANCIAL CAPITAL
For the first capital, Financial, I direct you to read-up on financing for your business from people with far more experience than me. There are literally hundreds of books out there on this subject, and for the majority of my MDP

audience, this is not something that they typically have much influence over, neither is it a part of their work. Financing the business is normally done long before our managers come on board. So for the sake of this chapter, we will leave this one alone.

HUMAN CAPITAL

That's me and you, along with all our intellect, our knowledge, our ideas and experiences.

One of the great challenges of managing a business is to think with our intellect rather than with our emotions, and for many in the hospitality industry, this is beyond difficult. We would rather think with our hearts, our intuition, than with logic and reason. One example that we like to work through is this:

Our employee is an entry level worker who has been employed with us for 5 years at entry level. Each year he has received an increase for his service to the business, unfortunately, though he is super dedicated to the business he just cannot be promoted beyond the entry level job.

This employee has just proposed an ultimatum to management. Either he wants a raise or he will resign. This is a classic challenge of emotion vs. organization.

Emotionally we have a dedicated employee whom we all know and love to have around the place. He is loyal after all and a part of the furniture. If we give him an increase/salary raise, we will get to keep him longer and we will not have to hire someone new.

Organizationally thinking, we have an employee who has reached the top end of the salary range for that position, the amount that the company should pay for an entry level employee, and now this is an opportunity to lighten the payroll and hire someone new at entry level who may have the potential to grow in the company in the future.

What do you do? I hope you go with the organizational decision. The problem is, if we look at a lot of businesses, they have consistently gone with the former, keeping people long past the time when they should be employed in their role.
Human capital as a topic is so rich, there are shelves filled with books on the subject. What we touch on here is hiring and retention. Hiring is so critical to success in hospitality that we dedicated a whole chapter to it later on in the book.

Perhaps the biggest part of the manager's human capital is building up love and trust and respect between his people. Extracting greatness: think about a fruit, how do you get the most out of it? Taking juice from a fruit means that there will have to be some cutting, some squeezing, and parts that looked good and wholesome at first will be thrown out in order to obtain the sweet nectar that we crave. Parts of the fruit may be used for creating other products, like jam, and some parts of the fruit for compost, yet other parts as seeds for future trees, and some, for that juice that is so full of goodness. This is the role of every great manager, to use every part of their people for the purpose that it best fits.

Great managers let people share great ideas. They keep out of the way of great people and enable them to perform. The greatest managers invest their capital in making amazing places for talented people to perform. The managers' job is to NOT slow down the people.

SOCIAL CAPITAL
Our social capital is our reputation, our relationships, our connections and trust.
Social capital is based upon one simple tenet:

DWYSYWD

Do What You Said You Would Do.

Oh, how I wish this were the norm, the standard. If everyone would do what they said they would do, most of our emails and communication meetings would be reduced to zero. The problem is that they don't. Start by you DWYSYWD! Your social capital will soar.

DEPARTMENTAL CAPITAL
Managers influence their operations by their presence and their personalities. They create a team that resonates with their style of leadership and that feels an affinity for the way a particular manager works. This is powerful stuff. It is not a capital that you can see on the balance sheet, but it is certainly one that will affect the profitability of your business. We want managers that are aware of their ability to influence the health of their departments for good; that are trained in the arts of motivation and delegation so that they make the whole team feel good. We want managers that excel in training their people that feel for the team, and

know how to leverage their team members by the way they talk to them.

CUSTOMER INFLUENCE

Our managers are the key to how customers feel about our businesses. Each manager can make or break the business. We frequently see that managers are the bottleneck in business, a great manager loves what he does, cares for the company and reaches out to the customers in a wonderful way, and they act as owners and extend themselves in every way to every customer, all the time.

Suppliers are customers, and managers must contribute by meeting and knowing the suppliers. The better your relationships with the people around you, the better your business deals. Foster good friendships that are underlined by good deals. Treat suppliers like customers and encourage them to be a part of solving your issues.

MATERIAL CAPITAL

Equipment is a key area of work. Simple rules to abide by are:
   a. Buy good quality in the first place
   b. Get plenty of quotations
   c. Take your time to think carefully and avoid time based deals that pressure a decision
   d. Take good care of equipment once you have it

You get what you pay for! I am always amused by the surprised behavior of people who buy cheap stuff and are surprised when it fails. What did they expect? At the same time, it s not always true that the most expensive is the best either, and that is why several quotations will help with this. It has never been easier to access information and so knowing the options available is merely a question of mastering search.

The challenge of suppliers is that once they have you on their lists, they will exert pressure on you to buy their product. They will offer you deals that on the surface may look very good, however take your time to think through the entire lifecycle of the purchase and make sure that further down the line it will still be a good deal.

If you are asking difficult questions, then you will probably find that there is no easy answer, and that if you are challenged by the question, so will most of your suppliers be. Take time to think it through.

Once you have gotten your equipment, take great care of it. Fix it as soon as it is broken. The day that it breaks, get it repaired. It's rather like my old Land Rover in Africa many years ago. The roads out there were so rough that your car was literally shaken to bits along the journey. If you left one thing to break, you suddenly found that you had a list of twenty things that needed fixing. At great pain I realized, fixing things as soon as they break is the *only* way to go.

Make sure that the team is trained to use equipment properly. A lot of equipment breakdown is avoidable by showing people how to use equipment properly *before* they start to use it.

Preventing breakdown rather than repairing broken things is a superior way of operating. Monitoring machinery and equipment and having rigid maintenance/repair schedules is vital to ensuring that equipment gives good service when you need it, and that it lasts its full lifetime. Ensure that as you buy your equipment, you install a preventative maintenance schedule.

Back to my original question then, "Why Capital x 4?" Because we multiply all of our capitals in different ways to achieve greater value than that of the original investment. A restaurant chain recently sold 18 outlets for $100M. That's a lot for 18 locations. The business had begun with just 1 outlet!

<u>Capital x 4 + Smart Work + Sales - Expenses</u> = Profit
Luck

SMART WORK

The heart of every successful hospitality operation is filled with hard work. Lots of people work hard. Many work long hours, and that is understandable, but frequently the management gets lost on this point. They think that if they are working long hours then they are adding value to the business. Mostly they think hard work is important because they grew up in the business and hard work is the culture of hospitality companies: You must work hard to succeed, and if you don't, then you are not going to.

This is fine to a point, yes, hard work is certainly important, and forms the building blocks of our future growth.

SW - Smart Work vs Hard Work

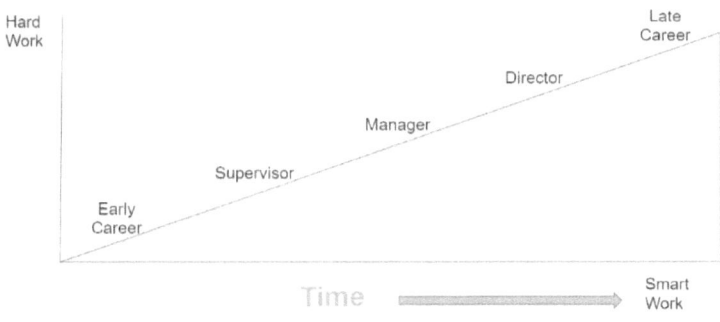

I think that this chart explains it perfectly. When you start off in this business almost 100% of your time is dedicated to hard work. As you grow you begin to work harder with your mind and less with your body. Finally work is made up of using your brains. Unfortunately a lot of people get stuck somewhere about 30% along the chart and even though their titles change, their head stays where they were.

Hard work is to do the jobs asked of you without really questioning or challenging the why. You put in a lot of hours and you are physically tired. You cook, you wash, you clean, and you serve. It is important to the overall understanding of the business, and if you skip this phase of the business, you will never quite understand later on in life what it means to be a laborer in the business.

Smart work is knowing what you want, why you want it, focusing on it, and going and getting it. Putting you as your priority and managing your time. You create your own deadlines, generate new projects without being asked.

Smart work is creating goals that you believe in, for yourself and for your team. Smart Work influences others.

The smarter we work the more influence we exert. We measure twice and cut once. We ask for great help, being overt in getting our needs met, and we copy great people that have already gone the way that we are trying to go (covert). We find the best people that we can to learn from. We get five great people around our life.

Smart work involves thinking about our business in intelligent ways.

Employee productivity is Smart work.

Example 1:
Total number of customers served/Total number of employees working = productivity

100 customers/10 employees = 10 employees per server

Example 2:
Total revenue for meal period/total number of hours worked = revenue per employee

$3500 revenue/ (10 staff * 6 hours) 60 = $58 revenue per employee

Both of these equations produce a number that can be useful in measurement. It can be used as a benchmark between different sizes of outlets and different types of operations to compare revenue per employee or number of customers served per employee. These are incredibly helpful numbers when looking at how your business is performing. This leads me to THE GOLDEN NUMBER

THE GOLDEN NUMBER

This is an optimum output from any given situation. Your average daily rate (ADR), your revenue per available room (REVPAR). What is a perfect day in your business like? How many employees should you have on duty? How many do you have?

The answer to this question is this:

The <u>least</u> number of employees to give the customer <u>our level</u> of service to our standards, making 100% of our customers happy.

This requires study. Study all of our business opening hours over extended periods of time to understand how many employees are actually required to deliver our standards. This will give us a formula that we can follow, which is called the GOLDEN NUMBER.

If breakfast can be served by 3 employees for occupancy of 65% and every customer is happy, then that is the GOLDEN NUMBER.

To figure out the GOLDEN NUMBER in every outlet and department of the operation takes time and study. It will not appear all by itself. It requires work.

Set up the quest for the GOLDEN NUMBER and get managers to compete to get it. Provide a reward and a prize and watch teams go after it. Once you have discovered the GOLDEN NUMBERS then you can create competition between outlets and departments. You can analyze the difference between brands.

Importantly these numbers can form the basis of a manager's bonuses in meeting this number, remembering all the time that the number guarantees the standards are met at all times. The interesting thing about these numbers is that over time, through fierce competition, managers will refine the numbers and attain better financial results while maintaining service standards because they believe that they are working towards a great goal.

$$\frac{\text{Capital} \times 4 + \text{Smart Work} + \text{Sales} - \text{Expenses}}{\text{Luck}} = \text{Profit}$$

SALES

The best way to solve a business problem is to go out and sell. All problems come from lack of cash. Go make sales, problem solved! Not really, but often. When it comes to being profitable, growing the profit can be done by increasing the sales per customer served. It is powerful and effective. Adding value to a sale that already exists, with a customer you already have is the best dollar you can add to your profit.

What if I were to tell you that you can be 75% profitable in your business? You would most likely say I am crazy; let's take a look and see if it can be done. You may be surprised.

100 customers a day in your outlet?

Average spend of $25 per customer.
Total revenue = $2500
Profit = 20%

Good business right?

But what if we encourage every one of those customers to spend $3 more in our outlet during their visit?

Growth of business = $300 for the day. That is a revenue growth of 12%.

If our costs on our sales are 25% for materials, then our profit would grow by cash $225.

That would be a whopping 75% profit on the additional revenue, and our overall result would be 25.8% - that's outstanding business. Super intelligent.

This process is down to training our team to add one more item to a customer purchase. You see, your general costs of employees, lighting and production are already in place. One more item for an existing customer means only the cost of goods for that product is required. What more could we ask for?

Add one more = multiplying profits. 75% profit

In order to prepare to do this activity we must monitor the average check for our business. Lunch, dinner, food, beverage and other. Break down the revenue into segments so that our team members will be able to understand the numbers. Make easy to read charts so that comparisons can be made and develop a reward system. Watch your revenue grow!

$$\frac{\text{Capital} \times 4 + \text{Smart Work} + \text{Sales} - \text{Expenses}}{\text{Luck}} = \text{Profit}$$

EXPENSES

Expenses have their own special formula, and it goes like this:

$$E = JE + RE + CE - BI$$

Our P&L and balance sheets are packed with numbers. Things that at first glance are just big numbers. What we have to do as managers is be able to break things down all the way to the last penny. Through this formula we can begin to categorize every single expense, and here's how we do it:

$$\text{EXPENSES} = \text{JUSTIFIED EXPENSES} + \text{RIDICULOUS EXPENSES} + \text{CARELESS EXPENSES} - \text{BRILLIANT IDEAS}$$

Justified expenses need no explanation. These are things that we cannot do without. We want to sell a steak, so what do we need? We need meat. Logical and intelligent expenses are those that are incurred in order to make our customers happy. They have a direct impact on customer happiness and the customer experience. They make it better.

$$E = JE + RE + CE - BI$$

RIDICULOUS EXPENSES

Here we want to emphasize that every single expense is paid out of revenues. It is key for employees to be taught the relationship between a sale and revenue. When a dish is ordered incorrectly by a waiter, the waiter feels no pain. It was just a mistake. Until that is, you come along and share the following:

COST OF A WRONG ORDER

Wrongly ordered item has a revenue of $25 and a food cost of $7

Wrong ordering of the dish will cost $7 food cost, + time of kitchen & production @ 30% = $8

Total cost of wrong order $7 + $8 = $15

If an item sold for $20 has a profit of 15% then the profit on that item is $3

The total sales required to cover the loss incurred by the wrongly ordered item is $100 or 5 dishes.

This is massive! One wrong ordered item needs $100 revenue to cover that loss... the goal? Zero wrong orders!

COST OF A BROKEN PLATE

Let's say that a nice restaurant dinner plate costs $4 to buy. Add to this the cost of contacting the supplier, the time of the person who has to do that job, it includes the cost of the phone call and emails, the purchase requisition that has to be signed, the cost of the store man to receive a new plate into the store, sign for the plate, send the delivery note to accounting, accounting to receive the invoice and match it with the purchase order and delivery note, enter it into the accounts, raise payment for the plate to the supplier, contact the supplier to let him know that his payment is ready, or to make a transfer, and then the costs of storing a number of spare plates in case another one gets broken, cleaning up broken plates, disposing of the broken plate. Now our broken plate has reached a cost of $9.

The broken plate is a loss of $9

The item that we sold for $20 with a profit of 15% will have to be sold three times for a revenue of $60 to cover the broken plate.

Therefore, one broken plate = $60 revenue! Not cool.

Other ridiculous expenses are using 2 garbage bags when one will do. Using customer napkins to clean up dirt instead of a paper towel. Coming late to work and still getting a full salary. Leaving work early and still getting a full salary. Employees ordering and eating customer food. Breakage of equipment. Damaging the premises by employees. Poor handling of equipment within the workplace. Hurting our customers by giving poor service.

SOLUTIONS?
Train our managers to train our team members on the cost of breakage and the relationship to sales. Everything that is broken has to be paid out of profits. Watch out! Get everyone to work together to get these things under control.

$$E = JE + RE + CE - BI$$

CARELESS EXPENSES

Managers that carelessly hire the wrong people create major expenses for our business. Managers that fire employees cost us a lot of money. Wrong discipline costs business a fortune. Poor coaching creates a void.

Over Empowered employees who throw away useful things suck a business dry. Those who act without integrity and who use the company's resources for their own gain are a drain on the business. This is what I call mismanagement.

$$E = JE + RE + CE - BI$$

BRILLIANT IDEAS

In a lively business that is well run we have lots of ideas all the time. Brilliant ideas come from our team members. Show them that they are important and that you want to listen to them. Ask employees what management does wrong, they know. Ask them where we are making mistakes and they will tell you. Employees know where we can save money and where we are losing money. They can help us to make more money than we ever dreamed of. Just let them know that you are on the lookout for great ideas.

AQAL is the key to finding these ideas. Ask Question and Listen. We rarely properly listen to our employees. If we find the time to listen, then we will find the time to learn from them.

ASK WHY?

The more that we dig, the more likely we are to get the real answer. Most frequently we are too lazy to ask the right questions. We ask a surface question, get a quick answer and at the end we know no more than when we started. By digging deeper and asking why? We will begin to know more.

And after we hear the first answer, then ask again the same question, why? The first time you do this people will look at you strangely, but do it again and you will cause a thinking process to happen. Now you will get a better answer. Then you ask why? Again and you will be much closer to the truth of the matter, and also you will draw closer to a brilliant idea.

Brilliant ideas can come from technology. New solutions are being created every day, there are millions of apps out there that can help in every area of life. Look at basic things like how people walk around a room, and the circulation in your outlets. Take the time to learn about new equipment in the market and new products that can grow your ability to provide better customer service with less cost.

Think about how you can offer the same services that you provide now, but with a reduced operation cost, rather than just looking at the prices. Improve profit through cost mindfulness. Tirelessly focus on the supply chain and think hard about the costs.

$$\underline{\text{Capital} \times 4 + \text{Smart Work} + \text{Sales} - \text{Expenses}} = \text{Profit}$$
$$\text{Luck}$$

LUCK
It was famously said by many, the only place where success comes before work is in the dictionary. And Ray

Kroc, the founder of McDonalds said that luck is a dividend of sweat. The more you sweat, the luckier you get.

You can beat luck by intelligence. Great systems beat luck.

Actually, one thing I have learned, and that has surprised me the most in life is this: if you set goals every day, and you are thankful. You give, you love people. You serve people. Then your luck increases. Things just get better and better.

At the end of the day, this formula is about PROFIT

You get what you focus on, so focus on what you want.

What I mean is this. A lot of people talk. They look good. They want us to believe that they have it all together.

Personally, I just don't believe it. Everyone is struggling with something. Jim Carrey said, "I wish that everyone could be rich and famous so that they would get it out of their system". No matter how well you are doing, there are realities in life that you cannot escape.

The reason is that MOST people are not focused. Mostly they are not focused on being profitable. MOST people are focused on silly issues that mean nothing rather on building a great organization.

Profit fuels the growth of the company, not turnover.

Profit builds the future. Focus on Profit. End of story!

8 MASTER SALESMAN'S TOOLBOX

Selling takes many forms. Sometimes it's something funny that sels you on a product, sometimes its sarcasm, most often, it's because someone else tried a product and you trust that person, so you go for it because they did.

Selling is a mind game.

Why do you buy?
What makes you do it?
Why do you go where you go?

I remember learning quite some time ago that the shortest course on sales is just one word:

AQAL

And ever since that day I have been an addict.

ASK QUESTIONS AND LISTEN.

I believe that everyone can sell, and in our courses we ask people to pick up any object and sell it. What's really funny is that we have just said that the best way to sell anything is by asking questions and listening, but what happens? Everyone starts by talking and trying to sell their product to the other person. They try all kinds of ways, but rarely do they listen.

Selling is a game. I love to sell. But there are super important rules to the game. Once you sell once, you will become an addict. The feeling of selling something is outstanding. You walk away with a great sense of achievement. It becomes addictive. Sell once, and you will want that rush again. That surge of good endorphins is tantalizingly addictive. The problem is, you have to sell more the next time to get the same feeling as the first time.

There has been much said about the skills and qualities of sales people and there are basics that are a must.

1. Looking the part counts a lot - make sure that you have your game face on, or your game voice ready
2. Listening and patience - don't talk while your prospect is talking - LISTEN
3. Knowing all about your product - have great knowledge, and not just about the product, but about life too
4. Trust builder - be someone that has a great handshake, from the first moment that the client shakes your hand, look them in the eye and smile and make them feel good. Never lie, people can feel it.
5. Strong enough to take rejection without giving up - a lot of sales calls end up as "no". The prospect is not going to buy. Don't give up. Instead of taking their "no" as meaning "no", take it as meaning "not yet".
6. Positive - always looking upwards, optimistic
7. Magician - able to work a little magic into every situation, be it a phone call, a face to face meeting, let people sense some mystery from you… don't give away everything in one go
8. Hard worker - sales are attained by those who work hard and who stay focused. Hard work brings it home. If sales were so easy, why, everyone would

be doing it and making millions. Sales is only easy for those who are totally dedicated to the process

9. Financially aware - make sure that what you sell makes sense financially to the business. There are hundreds of books out there that talk about what products to sell. Think hard and make sure that your product is attractive to customers, but also a win for your business.
10. Enthusiastic - giving personality - PASSION - you work hard to smile and be giving, loving and serving during the sales process. It starts from the first phone call, to the parking attendant at the building, to the lobby employees, the receptionist (especially), through the meeting, including anyone that serves you with coffee/tea/water etc. Say thank you to them out loud! And all the way out of the building and in the follow ups. The reason for that is you do not know the relationships between all the people that you meet along your way to the sales meeting and the person you are pitching to. The parking guy is probably a very good friend of your prospect, and may even talk about you to your prospect. Being the product all the time is the simplest way to be sure that you are doing right.

If we are to talk about customer service in hospitality then we are going to focus on some really important points that employees often forget.

CUSTOMERS COME TO RESTAURANTS TO EAT AND ENJOY THEMSELVES

A lot of times service personnel totally forget this. They got locked up in their own world of the place that they work, that they forget that service is all about making customers happy. Over-ambitious employees pushing to reach a goal are obnoxious and annoying and often sell less than genuinely caring employees. Recommend what is best for a customer and he will buy without being pushed.

Service is the most important part of selling. Follow up once you have sold your product to your client so that they will feel good about what they are buying and will come back for more, and they will bring their friends with them.

If you prepare well, then you can sell well. How you approach your customer is key to getting them to buy. We recommend that you write a sequence of service for all service personnel so that they know what they are supposed to say and how to say it. You can video it so that you have a wonderful template for your team members to follow, and you will build up the sale directly as a consequence of doing things right. What we think works best is to perfect your sales pitch, so that every team member knows how we do what we do (Done! Our training company is great and helping you to do this!).

Sales is about being observant. Watch arriving customers and try to figure out what kind of person they are and why they are here. Watch their body language, are they laughing and happy, serious and focused. As you observe their behavior work hard to match ourselves to how they are behaving. Happy customers demand lively sales people, serious customers expect focused and efficient sales people.

Have your sales pitch ready; don't show off, speak slowly and clearly and start your pitch.

When preparing your pitch you need to build in the following:
> Why the customer is here
> How much you think that they can afford to spend
> How time they have

Observing and asking the right questions will help you to be appropriate.

You may ask customers questions like, "Are you here for a quick lunch today?" This question will help you understand how quickly you must serve and whether you should sell right from the beginning or you will have time later on to grow the sale.

Your questions engage customers into a conversation, and conversations build up a relationship between you and your customers. Asking how they are doing today is a good one, because the majority of customers, even if they are having a tough day will answer this question for you.

When you ask, you also get the customer to share themselves with you and this shows interest, while giving you some control over the situation.

SUCCESSFUL SALES PEOPLE ASK GREAT QUESTIONS AND LISTEN

Throughout my whole process of serving customers I have come to know one very important lesson: Customers talk a lot of nonsense. They invent fictional lives to tell waiters and servers. They will tell you all kinds of stories about their adventures and possessions, all of this talk is designed to impress you! Yes, You! Customers like to impress their servers.

At the same time, customers like to ask questions, most of which fall into one of two categories. Customers will ask about the product. They will ask all kinds of questions about the ownership of the place, all the way across to local places of interest nearby. Be ready!

The other kind of question is about you. Customers like to ask servers questions, like, "Where are you from?"

If you want to sell, it is very important to answer this question well, and with lots of energy. A lot of servers are grumpy and find customer questions an annoying intrusion. They don't answer well and leave customers with a weird sense. You see, waiters love to get tips, and complain when they don't, but one thing that amazes me is how few waiters draw a direct line between how they talk to customers and the amount of tips they receive.

The product is prime.
You must know your product, food menu, drinks menu, ingredients, basic methods of preparation, and the services that your business offers.

Every employee that serves a customer must believe in why they are a part of the company and they must be sold on what the company does.

SUCCESSFUL SALES PEOPLE KNOW THEIR PRODUCT PERFECTLY

We spend a lot of time on confirming the sale, Making sure that we have understood what a customer has ordered. The best way to confirm is a simple echo technique, reflecting back to a customer what they have ordered as they order it.

Then deliver what you have promised.
　　　　　　　　　Crash. Bang Clang.

This is the point where so many restaurants and service establishments fall. From a simple glass of water being forgotten all the way to main courses that have been forgotten in the kitchen, the server is the master of ensuring that a customer receives what they have ordered.

I AM THE PERFECT SALES PERSON
I love to get people to write down who they think they are. I would ask you to do the same. Write down three words that describe who you think you are. Go ahead, you can write them right here

1
2
3

Now having written the down, I would say one thing: You are right! That is who you are!
In this generation everyone has an opinion about everything and they like to share it everywhere. Well here's my deal, you are awesome as you are. Perfect! Just the way that you are. Seriously. Don't let anyone tell you

otherwise. Now we may try to improve how you portray yourself at times, but actually, you are perfect as you are. And don't forget it.

The billboards and the TV ads, and the ads appearing all over social media tell us that we are not yet good enough because we don't yet have such and such a product. Nonsense. You are perfect as you are.

Stop now and say out loud, "I am PERFECT as I am"

Yes!

We don't want you to be someone else. We want you to be your greatest. At your current personal best. To shine. To be amazing. So remember, I am PERFECT as I am is the unbeatable statement.

In selling it is useful to understand a little bit about how people think. Our world is psychological, and we get by a lot of the time by watching what others are doing and doing actions similar to the current norm around us. We desire to fit in.

Clever advertising causes us to desire to fit in with a norm that includes the advertisers' product.

LIFE PATTERNS

Most people live in patterns. They follow along a pattern of pretty much what they have always done. They find a place that fits them and come back to it over and over again. So often people go on holidays to the very same place that they have been to before. I always ask myself, "Why?" Because they live in a pattern. They know that this pattern gives them a certain result and so they have become conditioned and created a tradition.

When you see two Lebanese people greeting each other, they know how to kiss each other and they know when. They know with whom they should kiss and with whom they should shake hands. That is a tradition. People follow others and do what others are doing.

SAFE BECAUSE IT'S POPULAR

Another sales force in action in people is the safety issue. We do what others have done before us because it has been proven to be safe. If everyone is doing it and they are living through the experience, then it must be safe for me. Once customers know that this is safe, they will repeat the behavior because it is safe, and so it keeps on going.

FAVORS

Returning favors is another human behavior that is great for selling. We are programmed for millions of years to give back when someone gives us something. It's a fundamental. Why do they give you a free sample to taste in a supermarket? Quite simply because you will rebalance the system by buying their product. They gave to you, so you give back to them.

SCARCITY

Scarcity is known to be a big sales building technique. That's why we see "ONLY 1 LEFT" and similar statements so often. You see, when something is scarce, it makes customers want it more. They have FOMO (fear of missing out), and they must have the scarce item. Tell a customer that there is only one more dish of the day available, you will probably sell it. Flash sales that state that they will end at a specific moment are the same idea. People feel that if they do not get a certain product or service by the time the clock runs down, then they will have missed out on a deal. Scarcity causes people to line up outside shops on cold January 1 to get a special bargain from a shop that claims to only have 1 of a specific item left and it is only going to be on sale at a certain price on a certain day. "I must get it!" cries the brain.

PAINTING PICTURES

One nice way to sell is to create a picture in the mind of your customers. BE ABLE TO DESCRIBE PRODUCTS SIMPLY. When you paint a picture of a product in your customers mind, they will want what you have told them about. Using words you can share about a product and customers will buy. As you describe you use words that create the feeling of pleasure and enjoyment from the dish that you are talking about, and use your open hands and open arms to explain.

GO WITH THE FLOW - INFLUENCE THEIR MINDS

When we explain that many others have bought this product today, customers feel a sense of safety about the product, but the thing is we can influence people's minds.

Derren Brown (a UK master of the mind and NLP and so on) talks about PWA. Perception without awareness. This is where people make suggestions about a product long before they reach the moment of purchase. Seeing a poster on the way to the zoo for the zoo, and especially the wonderful toys that you can buy of stuffed animals to take as a souvenir home with you, will have a very high impact on you as a customer at the zoo today. You are most likely to be attracted to buying a soft toy of an animal you saw at the zoo. Why, because the idea was planted in your head long before you got to the end of the zoo trip. Search for Derren Brown on YouTube and watch him in action as he influences people. It is a learnable skill.

A POWERFUL SECRET FOR GROWING SALES

There is a technique in sales called embedded commands. This is where we actually instruct a customer on what they are going to do. Does it work? You bet!

Here's how it goes.

Speak slower and use a lower voice. This is always more powerful and makes people pay attention. High pitched fast talking generates a different kind of emotion than the one we want here. What we want to achieve here is gaining full attention from our customers. Embedded commands are a combination of words and actions, and what this process actually does is disrupt neural pathways. During the disrupt you are going to instruct people to do something, and due to the disruption, they are going to grab a hold of something that will bring the disruption to an end.

Open your hand towards the menu, and with an open hand lean forward and tap the item on the menu with your palm facing the customer, smile and say,

> **"You are really going to enjoy this; it's our most popular dessert.**
> **Would you like to order one?"**

Now let's break this down so that you can understand what is going on here.

The open hand is powerful. It means, "don't be afraid of me, my hands are empty", there is no threat.

Smiling means I am not scary. I am not a risk factor.

Tapping the menu is a disrupt. Nobody taps the menu. It creates confusion in the mind of the customer and is unusual. This causes the brain to start searching for a way to normalize the situation.

You provide your customer with an instant solution to make this disruption go away, and that is the commands you have given them.

You are really going to enjoy this - it's a command = you are!
Enjoy = pleasure and increased happiness
It's our most popular dessert - it's safe. You are doing what others do, right choice
Would you like to order one? - It's a command = Order one!

Here's another example:

"Right now, most people choose this one"

This one is great. You are literally pulling in a sale with almost no effort. The best time to use this sales statement is when a customer asks what you would recommend. Again, you lean forward, open hand and tap on the menu on the item that you want to sell. You smile and say it.

Let's break it down:

Right now = when? Now! What? It's right! So this signals to the brain that this is the right choice for this moment in time
Most people = again right choice. Safety and popularity are in motion here
Choose this one = command. It is a direct command to the customer. It is done in such a nice way that it is hidden in our words.

Train your team on doing this and watch the results.

The key to all of this is to know what you want to sell and to believe in yourself. This technique starts off feeling scary. It is not easy to master, it takes practice. There are some really important body language tools that will assist in getting the sale completed, and these work not just in selling in a restaurant, they work in meetings in offices when you are trying to get your idea across and get people to sign up to your idea.

SMILE & STAND RIGHT
Smiling is critical to success. You see lots of big business people looking really happy. They have an aura about them. They seem to project happiness and success. It is down to how they stand and the control they have over their facial expressions.

Smiling starts a chain of goodness, so be the first to smile. Prepare your smile before you go into the room. I practice mine in the car mirror before I get out of the car on my way to the meeting. Then I practice my smile on the way to the meeting by smiling at random people on the way to the meeting. If there is a gatekeeper (receptionist) then I smile a lot as I talk to them. Smiles are contagious and memorable. The person you smile to will feel a sense of wellbeing and will extend your goodwill back to you when anyone speaks of you. By the time I enter the meeting room I am bubbling with goodwill and smiles. If I have a challenging meeting to go to where I am required to negotiate something difficult, I begin my preparation the day before, visualizing the meeting and me being calm and smiling while everyone is getting their head around the problem. With this mindset I walk into the meeting and my greetings are warm and genuine and full of power and smiles.

I stand tall with my shoulders back and a communicate goodness.

As a sales person I stand tall at the table, I smile and I look good. The smile is contagious and the customer will smile back. Genuine smiles are the key, not a grin like an idiot or clown. There are lots of ways to induce genuine smiles in yourself. You can practice in front of a mirror, it really works well. You can make a massive fake smile and then after your genuine smile will automatically appear because your brain makes fun of you which amuses you and makes you smile.

You can stand on one leg. It makes you smile. Hug a colleague. Make a loud noise. All of these actions will help you to smile.

NOD
The power of a nod is great. It shows that you are listening. When you nod and listen it shows that you care. Automatically people feel more comfortable with you as you listen to them. The nod puts the customer in charge. The customers will feel that they are directing the action and combined with your smile it encourages the customer to pursue their desires. Your nod shows your agreement with what they are selecting and this is very positive.

SAY "YES" A LOT
There are lots of books written on this topic, and there is no secret to the fact that if you get customers to say yes to small things, you can progress them to saying yes for more things. The problem with this theory is very simple, most people don't do what they know!

EYE CONTACT
Look into your customers eyes. Now there are some cultures where I have worked where looking into the customers' eyes is not encouraged as it symbolizes arrogance. Asian cultures have varying degrees of importance over eye contact. In western culture making eye contact is a good thing and encourages a spirit of positivity. Avoid staring! As a salesperson we can observe stress in a customer by their blink rate, if a customer is feeling stressed they will often blink more rapidly. Notice this and you know that it is time to back off and back pedal the sales level.

GENERAL SALES BODY LANGUAGE
Be natural. Find your own natural pose and work on it. Being yourself is important, but remembering that a strong

stance and positive position will make a difference means that you will need to learn a new natural stance to be able to be a better salesperson.

ENTHUSIASM
Be enthusiastic about what you are doing and most of everything we have talked about will come naturally. Enthusiasm and passion are critical components to being successful.

CONFIDENCE
We talk about it over and over, know what you are going to say, know what you are going to. Practice it until it is a reflex. You want to be good at sales, then practice. When should you practice? With every customer. The more you are aware of the process, the more you can use it with each order. You will be able to measure what works for you and refine it.

Combine all of this together and you will be an outstanding salesperson. Communicate this to all your front line team and you are going to see your sales grow.

SOFT SELLING
Soft selling is a constant presence in our processes. This is the skill of adding a few small items to the customer's order without setting off any alarms. We do not want to make our restaurant or business overpriced because we oversold the point where people perceive our price point and value. If the average check is $35, then our sales techniques should keep the price to within $38.50, about 10% more than usual. Soft selling, adding one more item, will achieve this goal and will prevent a salesperson from appearing pushy.

The soft sell is a smooth process of making the most of a golden opportunity presented by the customer. Why we soft sell is very important, it goes back to our on hospitality relativity and money. If you add one more sale to an existing customer you only have the cost of goods of the additional product to add to the costs of the business. Therefore the profit margin of the extra item is very high, as much as 70%.

To be successful in soft selling we have to know our product perfectly. The difference in selling is based upon how well the server is paying attention to the customer. The server must see the gap in the customer's order where a small item can fit in.

ONE MORE - ADD FRIES
The most successful upsell in history is the fast food industry's "large size?" whenever you order a burger. Learn from them!

Would you like fries with that? Is another effective sales line. Most people like fries. Maybe your business does not sell fries, but there is always going to be that one small product that you can suggest. Figure out two or three items that you can always sell and get your team members to offer that item.

Water is always a good upsell. Wait until the customer has finished ordering everything, and then ask them if they would like water too. Still or sparkling? Large or small? And in the Middle East we ask, Cold or Room Temperature? This series of questions becomes a process that develops tens of thousands of dollars of profit a year.

WOULD YOU LIKE ONE MORE?

Here we are able to sell more drinks, but this skill requires a lot of focus. You must first see that the customer has almost finished or completely finished their drink. While their glass is virtually empty you want to reach out with an open hand and nudge the glass slightly, smile and say, "Would you like one more?" If you do it in time, meaning almost before they are finished with their first drink or just after they have finished it, they will normally order another one. If you come back to the table too late, say after the customer has consumed more than 25% of their main course, they will not want to have another drink and you will have missed the opportunity.

SHARING PLATES

These days a lot of customers are used to different cultures where dishes are frequently shared. When you propose a sharing plate to add to an order it is a warm feeling for the customers. You are growing the sense of belonging between the customers and the place. Propose a choice between sharing dish one and sharing dish two, and point to it on the menu. "Should I get some for you?" is a powerful selling line. GET SOME is the embedded command. FOR YOU makes it personal.

ESPRESSO

Coffee is not a question. It is obvious. Make it so. Approach the table and as you take dessert orders you say, "of course you will want to have coffee with that right?" Of course makes it seem very normal. You will = embedded command, and at the end Right? Emphasizes that this is right.

If you tip your head over you will be endearing, kids do it all the time and mostly get what they want. Try it out.

Now here is a very special technique that I teach to expert sales people. This is for those who have mastered the processes that we have already discussed.

When a customer does not order coffee from me, but they have ordered desserts, I wait until I have served the desserts, and then I come back to the table. I put on a puzzled look on my face and tip my head on the side and say, "Did I already take your order for coffee?"
Here the skill is to be a great actor. Your puzzled look is important. As though you are busy and you may have forgotten if you took the order or not. Customers respond in several different ways. Some say, yes, you did, but we didn't order any. The waiter smiles as though relieved and says, something like, "thought I was losing my mind! Did you order coffee?" And the order will appear! Some customers will say you did not take the order yet, and you get to move forward, "so what will it be?" and the order will appear. This is a concept to play with and to practice. You cannot do it all the time, you cannot do it with repeat customers. It demands intelligence and practice, but it is effective.

Overall, the soft selling technique is focused on building the average spend per customer by about 10% for the entire table, and not more. This is not a massive push. Here's how it works.

Let's suppose the average check is $35 in your restaurant

1 customer   Upsell $3.5
    Total Bill Goal $38.5
2 customers   Upsell $7 on the table
    Total Bill Goal $77
3 customers   Upsell $10.50 on the table
    Total Bill Goal $115.50
4 customers   Upsell $14 on the table
    Total Bill Goal $154

So you have to be thinking carefully what you upsell and not to oversell. The server must keep this in mind. If the salesperson did not sell during the order taking process, there are still lots of chances left. The point of sales machine is a great indicator for the server to be able to check where they have reached so far. Soft selling is not about getting the most possible out of a customer. It is about building the customer experience.

HARD SELLING

This is a totally different strategy and cannot be applied to most customers. This works when a customer has a powerful presence, a strong ego and a desire to impress. The customer wants attention and wants to be made to look good in front of his guests. Typically this type of customer is well dressed, or cool, and surrounded by fans and friends.

In the hard sell we use direct language that demonstrates power and excellent choices.

"We are going to make sure you and your guests have a great meal. Can we do something special for you?"

"My name is Mark and I am going to be serving you. May I know your name sir/Madame?" followed immediately by "nice to meet you me/s MS xxxxxxx".

By connecting with the customer's name and my name there is now a powerful bond that will be useful throughout the meal process.

Power customers need a lot of attention, constant follow up and reassurance.

We ask permission from them, "May I suggest something for you this evening?" and await their answer. They may respond that they know exactly what they want. You cannot be offended by the language or approach of the power customer. Nothing they say is about you. Everything that they say is about them. If they treat you as a lowly server that is there to do their will, it is not about you. Be the server that they need. You WILL be rewarded.

Find out what they like and build on it. Offer dishes of substance that are showy and expensive. If they retract a bit it means that their wealth is just for show and not for spending. But if they step up to the offer, then they are the genuine article. That is the green light to bring out the fine wines and the special stuff.

A funny thing about customers is that they love to impress. Even if they are only impressing the waiter, they like to impress.

We should be in awe of customers and all that they have to say. Just listen, smile and agree. You must remember that you have no ego. Put your ego aside and be there to serve. The more that you focus on serving the more fun you will have. If customers say no to your suggestions it's perfectly ok. You are just offering them things from our menu. A menu does not get angry when you do not choose items from it!!!

Here is an interesting fact that I came across some time ago (but I don't remember where). It says this

75% of customers move on because they don't feel looked after.

That is scary. Imagine if you had every customer you ever had. You never lost one. What would business be like? Amazing! You would not have enough space to take care of them. Teach your team to take care of customers. Make them feel cared for. Listen to them. They will stay. They will come back. They will bring friends.

CREATING MAGIC
At the end of all this there is one more secret to selling successfully. That is to create magic. We can do this by any number of things:

Anticipating customer needs - watching the table and clearing away used things or bringing things unasked

Being nice and warm. Being knowledgeable about products and able to talk about the food and drinks with the guests in a way that you are educating them and showing them.

Understanding the culture behind your concept so that you can share a bit about the ownership of the restaurant in a personal way that makes guests feel that they have connected with the restaurant.

All of these techniques create a wow moment for customers that they will always remember and that will attract them to come back.

DO IT
The sad thing about this chapter is that virtually all of my readers will get to the end of the chapter and do nothing about what they have read. Look, I will be honest with you, the refinement of service today is not about the table tops and the chinaware. It is about how you make people feel. It is all about creating amazing experiences for customers.

You must train and educate your team members to become the outstanding salesperson that grows your business. Very few restaurants ever achieve this. In my mind, even some of the Michelin star restaurants don't do this. They are technically perfect, but they do not capture your heart. You have an incredible meal experience in their place, but you don't feel connected forever. The memory drifts off into the past in a blur of similar experiences. The time when experiences will stick is when they were made personal. Then they become a part of your life. Rarely a Michelin star restaurant delivers what I call a personal experience.

Your restaurant deserves this level of attention and if you deliver it you are going to feel the difference in your customers.

Step 1 - train your people to these things
Step 2 - set goals for them to reach in terms of the upsell
Step 3 - display the results on the wall in the restaurant
Step 4 - give meaningful prizes for achieving results

Be personally responsible for delivering this training to your team and watch what happens.

9 SIT & WATCH

This is one of my favorite chapters. This is all about innovation, rejuvenation, and focuses on three key things: Analysis - Creation - Action.

Sit & Watch challenges what we do with our time. A lot of business owners are going through their business doing the same thing each day that they did the day before. This is going to give you pretty much the same results as what you got before. Frustration builds up so owners decide to hire in mystery shoppers. Why? To tell them what they cannot see for themselves. The fact is that this is a myth. Mystery shopping is laziness. I am against it and no one can convince me of its value.

The first problem with mystery shopping is the quality of personnel conducting the mystery shop. There are very few people who will take the time to truly understand the culture and spirit of the company for whom they are doing the mystery shopping. This means that as they go into an outlet or operation to conduct the mystery shop, they are going to be working from a basis of generic values that they associate to this standard of outlet. At best you are going to get a generic return.

The second problem is that you are paying someone to give their opinion. This means that they will have to deliver what they think is the value that they have been paid for. If they deliver a glowing tale, then what is the point in having hired them? If they tear the place apart then no one will want to listen to them. Back to square one.

The third problem is the resentment from employees and the wasted time that results from the mystery shopper. Team members will take time to go back and watch video camera footage to figure out who the mystery shopper is and to be ready for them the next time they come. An air of being caught insidiously slips into the organization.

Why do I say it is laziness?

A well run organization does not need a mystery shopper. It needs a constant eye on attention to details by its management, and ongoing training program for its team members, a rolling program of product development to move the product forward and keep it fresh, and regular and proper maintenance.

Over the years I have discovered that there is one remarkable way to overcome the mystery shopper myth and to create an incredible spirit of growth and motivation within an operation that gives power to owners and operators.

SIT & WATCH
Sit & Watch is a program that I created that is designed to give you all the feedback you need to have, and more. Here's how it works:

PREPARE YOURSELF
Before doing sit and watch there are things to be done. You must prepare. You will need a pen/pencil and paper. Not a digital device. This is so that you write things down and draw stuff without being distracted by tweets and bleeps

and messages and calls. Get rid of the phone. Silence and out of sight for the first 40 minutes.

TELL THE CHEF
The chef needs to know what is going on, otherwise you are heading for disaster. Take the chef aside and explain that you are going to be sitting in the restaurant on a very busy day in the middle of service to assess what is going on and to feel what the customers are experiencing.

SELECT THE BEST SEAT IN THE HOUSE
Here is where controversy starts. Sit & Watch is designed to understand what our best customers are experiencing, so that we can verify that this is what we want them to experience or to improve it. Most of our managers spend their time solving problems, moving around their outlet and generally taking care of stuff. They never experience the restaurant as a customer and definitely not in the busiest of times.

Let's just think about this. When do most of the problems come up? In the busy periods.
When do most of the customer complaints come up? In the busy periods
How often do we have the time to really look at the live service and experience it? Never!

That's why we do Sit & Watch. We go to the prime seat. The prime seat is where you can see the whole restaurant and where you can see everything that is going on in the entire place. You will have to book the seat in advance. Do it as per a customer process. This is the beginning of Sit & Watch.

Keep notes about the entire process. From the reservation to the arrival to the seating, everything that happens until you are out of the restaurant.

You cannot move from your chair.
You sit there no matter what happens. If you feel uncomfortable, good. That is what your customers feel like! Now you know how it feels.

If you see something wrong all you can do is write it down. You cannot go and fix it. You cannot give instructions to employees. You cannot tell anyone to do anything to fix anything while you are doing this process. You are a customer.

If your job requires that you wear a uniform, on this day at this time, you do not wear one. You dress like your typical customer does.

ORDER WHATEVER YOU WANT - Ignore any criticism. IGNORE ANY CRITICISM - no matter what your team members say about you doing this process, stick with it.

When I say order whatever you want, I really mean that. Order whatever you want. Wine wise, remember that you need to be sober enough to do your job, so don't overdo it and abuse, but do order some decent wine. Don't go for the house wine.

Now what do you do?

SIT & WATCH!

What are you going to watch?

I don't know!

What k nd of stupid idea is this, Mark?

THIS IS THE BEST STUPID IDEA YOU WILL EVER HAVE

Why?

Because we are all sick! We are desperately sick. We have an incurable disease. We are always doing something. We are busy. Either we are solving issues that we should have delegated to someone else a long time ago, but that give us a sense of importance, or we are ignorantly control freaks who have to be in charge of everything and constantly micromanage everything. Whatever it is, we are always doing something.

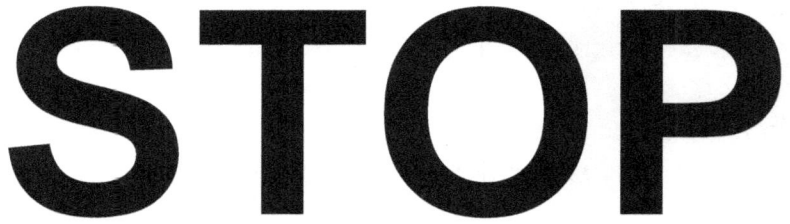

And SIT & WATCH.

What is your objective?

1. ANALYSE
2. CREATE
3. ACT

ANALYZE

Begin by watching everything that is going on around you and writing down anything and everything you see and feel. Good things, or bad things. Positive and negative. Think about why these things are happening without trying to solve them.

Sit very still and just enjoy the process of being served. By sitting still you are going to see a lot of things that you have never seen before. You will see things from a brand new perspective. You will have a different attitude, since you are obliged to stay in your seat and restricted from solving issues on the spot.

And what if you don't see anything new? Don't worry. This is the very reason that you are sitting here. SIT & WATCH only works when you SIT & WATCH.

If you go to the movies how long is your typical movie? All the greatest movies of recent times are at least 90 minutes to 100 minutes long.

SIT & WATCH IS 2 HOURS LONG

WHAT WILL YOU SEE?

Incorrect flow of staff; how often customers need service but no one takes care of them; the damaged paint on the corners; the stain on the floor; the light bulb that is not working; the fact that a table is badly positioned for a customer; the possibility to introduce more tables into the restaurant if it is more organized; cigarettes in the flower pot; torn apron of a waiter; cobwebs around the light fittings; stuff on a side station that should never be there; a tip box taking pride of place at the cashier counter; servers carrying stuff without a tray; hands on the rim of glasses when serving fingers on the plates as servers set them in front of customers; no smiles on the faces of servers; supervisors and managers hopping around but generally unproductive; more than one server caring for the same client; various different servers pouring wine for one table; no one upselling; can create a new plate that makes the presentation more exciting; think about adding more color to the offering; change the roles of servers; understand the true current training needs; create some new desserts to bring a sparkle; refine the table top equipment to be more elegant; add an envelope for the invoice to be given to customers after payment that acts like a business card and says 'thank you'; invent gift cards for customers to give away to their friends; have a dancer perform; have an app so that customers can create his own meal; special drinks offer for a reason; make everybody happy put marijuana in the recipe; figure how servers can be more happy in serving.

CREATE

The next step of SIT & WATCH is to make something out of nothing. To create. Remember Flow - Click - Think?

The things that you have seen become stronger the more that you look at them. Things come into focus. Solutions begin to roll in your mind. When you are doing your manager thing on a normal day, you typically see something going wrong and put it right. But is this a solution? No! This is called firefighting. You put out the flames for that moment, but you did not solve the problem.

During SIT & WATCH you are doing something entirely different. You are a different you. This you is sitting, looking, writing and thinking. The other you is reacting and moving.

Don't get excited yet. STAY STILL!

You will be about an hour into the exercise by now, and you should be getting served and so on. Do not move from your place. Do not start trying to solve issues. That will defeat the purpose of your exercise. You have not yet made the full journey to the end. You are only half way through. There is more to come.

WARNING - if you stand up and start doing your management owner thing, you will reset the clock and your activity is over.

So what should you do? STAY STILL, and

SIT & WATCH

Keep on searching
Keep on looking
Keep on writing
Keep on thinking
Keep on creating

ENJOY THIS MOMENT
You have now passed from the analysis stage. You are out of your critical mode and you have passed the shock of seeing all the things that are going wrong. Your mind has made a shift to the next phase where you are into creating new things. So enjoy the moment. It is a special moment

where you are now able to see things with a certain clarity. Can a mystery shopper give you this? NO WAY!

What comes next?

ACT
The final part of SIT & WATCH is to act. Do I mean right now? NO!
I mean look over all of your notes and circle the things that are a top priority. Your A list. The most important elements that will enhance and improve customer experiences. This is where you start your action plan.

There is no employee discipline as a result of this exercise. The reason? You are responsible my friend. You have personally created whatever you are experiencing. If you have felt downright uncomfortable throughout this whole 2 hours and you are frustrated, that is all frustration with yourself. You have allowed your operation to become what it is delivering right now. So grow up and look yourself in the mirror and say, "I will make my place a better place". If you feel the need to write out a warning letter for someone, address it to yourself.

Create an action plan of encouragement, building and growth. Set crazy goals that will take your business to a new level and improve everything about everything.

And that's it: SIT & WATCH

As you now know, it is simple. It is not easy!

A few thoughts about this process that may answer questions you have in your mind. One of the big ones that people often ask me is this: "Won't the employees know that I am doing a study of the outlet?"

Great question. At the beginning they will. But that will last for not more than 20 minutes. They can't act for longer than that. They just watch you writing stuff down, and as long as you don't blow it by engaging them in fixing stuff or directing them, and you do not engage in long conversations with supervisors or people on the floor while you are doing this, then you will be forgotten by your team as they perform their work for other clients. Remember, SIT & WATCH should be done on a prime day at the peak of service.

How often should you do SIT & WATCH?
You should do it in a newly opened outlet, an outlet that has been open for a long time, when you are getting lots of customer complaints, when you have a successful outlet, when you are not doing anything new and you feel a sense of boredom setting in, when work has become repetitive, when you are losing your focus on customer happiness or when things just don't feel quite right.

In reality you should probably do it about once every three to four months, not less than twice a year for each outlet that you have.

Do it personally. Don't delegate this task to someone else.

When you do SIT & WATCH try to be alone or with only one other person who is aware of what you are doing. It is not a group activity otherwise you will get distracted and end up in a meeting style format over a meal and you will become unaware of what is really going on. Alone is best.

WHAT IS SIT & WATCH?
    2 HOURS
    DON'T MOVE
    ANALYSE
    CREATE
    ACT

10 THE FINAL WHISTLE

You cannot manage time. Let's get this straight right from the start. Time moves forward regardless of where you are, or what you do. You cannot impact time and you cannot change time.

What you can do is manage what you do with your time.

What scares me about this chapter is that there is nothing I am going to say that you do not already know. And that is where the problem lies. We are so conscious of time and how quickly it moves, but we do not use it as we should.

You DON'T DO the things that you know you should do to manage what you do with your time.

I often talk to people and ask them how things are going. They say they are so busy. I ask them to you put a plan for what you are going to do every day. They smile, look at me as though I am stupid and say, no, I just told you I am so busy.

I look at them and smile and say, tell me when you have time to talk about it and maybe I can help you out. They always say yes, but I am still waiting for the phone to ring!

How should you manage your time?

Do yourself a favor and hop on over to bit.ly/1iq2iWK Mindtools.com have set up a very useful little tool over there that you can use to assess your usage of time. At the end of the questionnaire it will give you result. Fun to do right? But are you any better off than you were five minutes ago? I doubt it.

Google is one of the greatest inventions in the history of the world. It basically put the entire sum of all human knowledge at your fingertips, all you have to do is type in a simple phrase like "how should I improve how I manage my time" and you will get something like 427,000,000 answers. That's a lot of answers. That means that a lot of people are struggling with the same issue. Almost half a billion people have put up some kind of answer to this question, in one way or another. Write time management and you get a whopping 1.6 BILLION answers. So, yes, this is obviously an important topic.

I don't have all the answers, but I do have some cool answers that will improve your life.

Let's think about this carefully.

If we live until we are in our eighties, and you are somewhere around 30, it will mean you have something like 20,000 days left to live. That breaks down into about half a million hours of life to go. Interestingly you are going to spend about 120,000 of those hours sleeping.

This is serious time usage!

So how should you use your time wisely? This is the best question to ask.

WAKE EARLY

Wake up at a good time that allows you to start your day with a period of gratitude and thinking about the day ahead. If your first thoughts in the morning are all about what you are grateful for, it will start your day in a powerful way. Write them down in a notebook. Every single day. Sunday too. Take the time to think about all the things you are thankful for this day. Do it every day. Keep a note of the time you woke up. Do not touch your phone.

3 GOALS FOR TODAY
the last thing you write after you have written your thankful list, is to write down three things for today. This will guide your mind throughout the day. You can come up with some amazing stuff by yourself. Just make sure you do it every day.

WORK OUT
Every single day do some kind of body movement before you get going into your business. Taking care of your body is wonderful. It feels so good. You are proud of your shape and how your body feels. It makes you feel good. How long do you need to work out? It doesn't matter. Just do whatever feels good to you. But work out. Oh yes, keep a note of your work out and your weight.

Get these two things right and the rest of your day is going to be a success. I promise you.

SEE YOUR FAMILY
Spend time with your loved ones before you get out and about. Give them the first of your day when you are thankful and energized. Now we are rocking. Don't tell me you don't have time. This is all about managing what you do with your

time. Now you can open your phone. At first you will feel pain in not touching your phone. It will be playing on your mind. Discipline your phone. Let it wait until you are ready and have filled yourself up with goodness.

Think about this: Gratitude overflows into positive energy. Working out overflows with positive physical energy. Spending quality happy time with your family gets you positively focused. Now you are ready for your day.

YOUR WORK
Focus your time on getting done what you are great at doing. Get rid of everything that you do that causes you stress or frustration. Delete it from your life. Find someone to do it. You are going to tell me you cannot afford to pay someone to do those things. Maybe. But aren't you the person that 20 minutes ago told me that you are too busy to think about how you manage what you do with your time? :)

If you just focus on what you are great at doing, and living by doing what you are gifted at doing, your life is going to be a lot of fun. There is a whole world of life work to be done on this subject. We have an app for this that helps people to really get through from where they are to where they want to be in terms of using their time to do what they are really brilliant at, and shining day after day because their time is devoted to doing what they love. So many yearn to do what they love doing but don't do it. Take some serious decisions and say, I will give my life to doing what I love. Then find the way to do that.

Give time for work. Do work while it is time to work. Don't play on your phone. Close the apps. Get a double screen computer. It saves you hours of time because you can see two pages at once, or two things at once. Leave general emails to the end of your day.

Don't sacrifice your family time for work. Family is family. Be fully present. My family time is sacred. I do no work during family time.

WALK EVERY DAY
get out and walk for at least five minutes every single day of your life. Make it part of your day. These five minutes will give you a moment for yourself. It can be as simple as getting to the car, turning around and walking away for 2 and a half minutes, then turn back and return to your car. By doing this, wonderful things will happen. Just make sure that it is always a minimum of five minutes. Who knows? You may end up running a marathon!

SLEEP BY MIDNIGHT
Yep! Get to sleep on time. Get some proper sleep. Most of what you do after 11pm is useless to your life. TV is crap. Turn it off. News is garbage and adds nothing to your life. Don't watch it. It holds you back. Turn off your computer and go to bed. If you are going to tell me that you have to stay up to work then I am going to tell you that you have not yet figured out how life is supposed to be run. If you are working late at night it is because you are doing the wrong things during the day. And if you tell me that you have too much to do then you are a control freak with trust issues, because you are not getting others to help you do simple things so that you can do your best work at your best time.

Try giving away some decisions so that you can sleep on time.

Write down what time you sleep. The goal is by Midnight.

YOU ALREADY KNOW ALL OF THIS!

So what's' the problem?

You know what needs to be done, but you don't do it.

WHY?
When we have a disease we go to the doctor and he examines us. The doctor will then prescribe treatment for our disease and will expect us to comply. If the doctor thinks that the patient is going to ignore him, he hospitalizes the patient and sticks a drip feed into the patent so that they are now a prisoner of the treatment.

When our team members know what they are expected to do and they don't do it, we call them into a meeting and we challenge them to deliver exactly what we are asking and we expect immediate results.

Here is the diagnosis: YOU ARE SICK.

You are surfing books, internet, LinkedIn, Facebook etc. looking for the one golden bullet. The one thing that will fix everything. The problem is this, there isn't one thing that will fix it. There is a series of things under the banner of personal discipline; daily rituals.

Live right personally and life will become a joy.

Symptoms of your sickness

TIME WASTED IN YOUR OFFICE
Walking around when you should be sitting down working. Spending time with people chatting kills your productivity and theirs. If you have time to chat and kill time, they probably don't. You steal your time and theirs. And worse, you are stealing company time (which is money). So you have become a thief. At work do your work.

TIME WASTED IN OUTLETS/OPERATIONS
People who are always present are not productive. They want us to see that they are here and working hard, but actually they are not. You have created a system that is not productive and you have created a culture of burned out employees who are all pretending to be indispensable. You do not have to do EVERYTHING! Get your team to help you out and you will be able to work a decent number of hours.

POSTPONING DEADLINES
This is a failure by you. When you do not reach a deadline it is your failure because you did not manage what you do with your time. When you first received the project you had a discussion that went along of the lines of outlining what

had to be done. Then you entered a further discussion into how much work it would take and how long it would take. And finally you had an agreement to complete the project by a certain time and date. You not completing on time means a lot of things. Firstly it means that you are an annoying person to the operation. No matter how valuable you are, you are the cause of frustration. You did not do your work on time. I don't care why, I just care that you didn't do it on time. It means that you lack maturity to get stuck into your project when it was first assigned, so you did not understand how much was required and after just a few days come back to your business associate and explain what you have discovered about this project and share together a new and better deadline so that you can get help or deliver on time. You were arrogant and felt that the project could be done later and that you would be able to do it in the last minute. This is a disservice to the people for whom you were working, be they clients or management. You did not do the job to the level you could have done.

How do I know all this? Because I have done all this! When you deliver a poor project you know it. When you are late you know it. When you postpone it is because you were not ready on time, you know it. It means that you did not manage what you had to do in the time you had available. What you need to do is work out how many working hours a project needs, then add 10%. So say a project needs 30 working hours, we make that 33 working hours. Then we need to get our calendar out and think about how many hours we can work on a project at any one time, say two hours, so our 33 hour project will require 17 * 2 hours to complete. Now look at your schedule and fit in 17 two hour appointments, noting all of the commitments that you already have. Now you will have a true date by which you can deliver what was requested. Now add 2 days more to it and go back to your colleagues and explain that your delivery date for this project will be on such and such a date and here is why. You will always win. Either you will get the time that you have requested, or you will get help, or someone else will be asked to do the job. All ways, you win.

POTENTIAL VS. OUTPUT CONFLICT

A person with a high potential and a low output is a stress to an organization. High potential personnel must deliver quality output. Their productivity must match their potential. If it does not then it is time to have a sit down and talk. Load them up with more to do, figure out due dates (use the system above - for which we have an app), challenge them with fixed delivery expectations and a support network. Otherwise you need to sit down and figure out how this person is using the time that they have at the company and help them to use their time more wisely on the things that really count.

INTERRUPTIONS & YOUR PHONE (AGAIN)

Some people tell me that they are being interrupted every five minutes by someone or another. Control Freak! That is who you are. If you are being interrupted it is because you have created the system where people have to come to you for approval on a whole load of things. UC Irvine has produced a study that people switch tasks every three minutes and five seconds. 185 seconds between one interruption and the next. Importantly it takes 23 minutes and 13 seconds to get back to the task they were originally doing. Most people never get into doing any serious productive work. Back to the phone thing. Messages are an ever present interruption. Notifications keep on binging and bonging. Your phone calls you to tell you that you have a new email etc. etc. and takes control of you. Control it!

I put my phone on silent and keep it that way. When I start to do something important I just turn it over and on silent. I remove all notifications from apps like news and breaking news events.
My home screen is plain and has no apps on it so that when I look at my phone it is not calling for my attention. My phone works for me. I do not work for my phone.

There is a wonderful feature on virtually all modern phones, it is called missed call record. You can see who called you and you can call them back at your convenience.

Really, when you answer a call in a meeting it is a disaster. No one really cares who you have to talk to. Neither do they care what you are talking about. It is not important to them. So you hold up a meeting of other people because your ego says that you are more important than them. Sad. Reevaluate. Put the phone down so that it does not interrupt.

My phone works for me.

WAITING FOR AN ANSWER
Many times we are held up waiting for an answer from someone. If they are higher up the so called food chain we may be paralyzed waiting for them. Over time I have faced this on different occasions and I have frequently felt that I will not be well received for asking whatever I need to ask. One thing that often stands in the way of junior team

members getting what they need when they need it is the false images that they create in their minds of the person that they are going to ask from. I have heard people say things like they are afraid to ask for what they want because of... and then they create a bunch of myths about what this person may or may not be thinking or be like. Here's the bottom line on this subject: Don't let others create for you a block either real or imagined on your way to getting your job done. Ask for what you need, when you need it and listen to the answer. If the person will not solve your problem or provide what you need, politely inform them by email note or in person that what they have asked for from you will be delayed until you get what you need. Simply as that. Let them deal with their own issues.

I have observed office politics in many work environments for many years, and one thing I know is that people love to leverage for their own gain. People will sell you a story about someone that is totally not true usually for their own ends. Brush past it and go for what you want because you need it for the job you are trying to do. Most owners and reasonable bosses will respect you for this and you will have reputation for being someone who they can trust.

There is saying that goes like this, "The squeaky wheel gets oiled first".

NO TIME FOR A HOLIDAY
This is about the most ridiculous thing I hear managers saying. Rarely owners! Managers that cannot take a holiday are not managing properly. If you cannot leave your work to get reenergized, refreshed and refocused, then you are not a useful person to have on board. You are going to burn out

and it is going to create a crisis. The world can survive without you. It is a fact. It has been proven millions of time. Will things be done your way when you are not there? I don't know. But what I do know is this, it will go on. Same goes for days off. I want every manager to take their day off or their days off and come back ready to give 100%. They must be fresh and ready to give to their teams and the only way to do that is to take a break.

GYPSIES, VAGRANTS & WANDERERS
There are dangerous people out there and some of them work for us. They roam around the office seeking junk to collect. They gather up stories, make them bigger, drop them around the place and sometimes light fires in dangerous places and even set forests alight. The people always appear busy at the right moment, they make a lot of noise when they have something to do that has been asked of them by a so called important person. They will tell you all about what the important person has asked them to do, and they will probably shroud it in secrecy. These people are time thieves. They steal your time whenever they come your way.

In my experience they are hopelessly lost and there is no cure. Kick them out. Make sure that you do not lose or use your valuable time with them, ever.

RULE YOUR TO DO LIST
By having three clear goals for your day, you will by time find that you are able to achieve those three things that you set out to do, pretty much every day.

A lot of people come up with a to do list and they let it sit there and stare at them. They grow the list and occasionally cross something off it. This is a tyrannical list that will never end. It will rule you forever.

Here's what you need to do to overcome the TO DO LIST

RIGHT NOW WRITE DOWN ON A SHEET OF PAPER EVERYTHING THAT YOU HAVE TO DO.

No matter how long it takes, write it all down. Keep on working on writing it all down until you are completely done. The first column is the task to be done, the second column is the number of hours that the task requires and the third column is when you must be done by.

Here's an example:

TASK	NO OF HRS REQUIRED	DUE DATE
Write book	55*8 hours = 40 hours	31/8

The magic of disposing of your to do list is to now transfer this into appointments in your calendar. If you look at this task, it needs 40 hours of work. I know that I can focus for two hours at a time to do writing and then I need a break. Therefore I am going to need 20 different appointments to complete this task. So I open my calendar and I turn to 31/8, the date when I want to be completed by and I select a day two days before that, 29/8 and I enter a 2 hour appointment. Now I realistically work my way back crossing off my list the blocks of two hours that I will need to finish my task by that day. If I reach today and find that I have more appointments remaining that are unallocated, it means that I will have to step up the amount of time that I put into an appointment from 2 hours to 3, or more, or I will have to extend the deadline further. Once I have put all of these appointments into my calendar I cross the item off my list of things to do.

I systematically go through every single item on my to do list and move it into my calendar. My calendar is online, it is on my phone and on my computer and they are synced. There are lots of software that will do it, but both Apple and Android have this figured out really well.

Where is my to do list? Gone!

I am a free man. I look at my calendar and I am free to do anything I like with the time where I have no appointments. There are lots of those empty spots. What is wow about this is that whenever I have the opportunity for an appointment with someone I just ask them when they are free and I give them a spot on my calendar. I instantly add the appointment and I am done. My computer will remind me and my phone will remind me of the appointment if I want it to. Perfect.

No more list.

WHEN THE TIME COMES
Do it! The most important part of this system is that when the time for the appointment comes you must do the work that you have scheduled, or you will fall behind. This is all about self-discipline, which after all is the core of managing what you do with your time. Again, I cannot emphasize enough, turn off your phone when you go into an appointment to write a report or when you have given

yourself an appointment to do something. Do not allow yourself to be tempted to open email or messages or Quora or similar. Your time will be absorbed like a sponge and you will not finish the task assigned. So be like Nike. Just Do It!

Remember, most emails are crap. I can prove it. Don't answer any email for 5 days and see what happens. You will get some people that will call you and ask you for your answer to their email and the rest will just slowly become a deleted file.

If you do have to answer emails, most of them can be answered with a minimum number of words. Use less words. You can answer with one word, such as "noted" or "thanks"

THOUGHT POST ITS

When you are working on a task your mind will pop up some attractive (distracting) ideas. Use post it notes to capture those ideas. Just jot the idea down and then refocus on what you were working on. Don't go down the rabbit hole of discovering something new while you were supposed to be finishing the task at hand. The post its can be evaluated at another time and you can then disperse appointments to follow up on this new idea if it is worth it, or add it to a meeting agenda for general discussion as appropriate.

THE ADVANTAGE OF GETTING GOING

The beauty of this system is that it gets you going with your work in a timely manner and removes stress over deadlines. In fact you will feel at peace because you have a clear idea of what you are going to be working on. Another advantage is that starting right away will, as we said before, give you an idea of how much work there is involved in this project and that will help you to produce real quality work.

BACK TO YOUR TO DO LIST
When you have converted all of your tasks into appointments you will probably have some stuff to do that you don't know what to do with. These are bits and pieces and will probably be a phone call or a face to face chat with someone.

If you need to meet with a busy person then send them an email with options of when you are free and let them pick the time for the meeting. This will save you back and forwarding over a meeting and eliminate emails. When you get the time from them for the meeting, then send out a meeting reminder on everyone's calendar. Do it right away so that you do not create conflicts.

THE NONSENSE OF MEETINGS
Avoid meetings that are not required. If you are not required in a meeting then say so. And don't go.

If you need to have a meeting, then make the meeting for an amount of time that you really think it will require. Make meetings for 20 minutes, don't book a whole hour. Book long meetings as 50 minutes (Google Calendar is set up for that), this releases you ten minutes of time for each meeting. When you go to the meeting get down to business right away.

If you are in charge of a meeting that is regular and everyone arrives and obviously has not prepared anything and they are waiting to churn through the agenda, cancel the meeting. Let everyone go and be productive instead of grinding through a meeting for the sake of it. They will appreciate you more. And if they then come up to you during the following days looking for solutions then you will be able to coach them that the meeting was important and you will help them to see how they should prepare for a meeting by gathering all the things they need to get answers to from the meeting before they go.

In Tokyo we used to have standing up meetings. These were great. Everyone walked into the meeting, we stood in a circle, we went through the points that everyone had and we then left the meeting. It was super-efficient. Operations meetings work well standing up. There are lots of advantages, there are no status symbols, desks, blocks etc. and everyone feels a sense of urgency to get things done and move on.

Avoid setting up meetings far away, and if you are obliged to go, see what you can do on your way to the meeting or on the way back. A far away meeting eats your time so try to plan how to get to the meeting in such a way that you can be productive during the period of travel. Get someone to drive you if it is in a car and you work while they drive.

Try to get smaller meetings for decision making. There is a wonderful book about this called Parkinson's Law. Very interesting indeed. Avoid having hangers-on in the meeting. Just get the people together that you need in order to be able to finish what you have to do in the time that you have to do it.

Again the 50 to 55 minute time frame for a meeting is the maximum. Tell people at the onset that the meeting should be done by 10:50. If there are still things to discuss then reschedule them for another time and get out of the room. Why? If the meeting keeps on hanging on and on, the mood f ags and the energy leaks out. We have one exception to this rule and it is in our 70 BY 7 program, but that is another story in another book!

The last five minutes of the meeting is all about making sure that everyone knows what comes next in terms of deliverables and timelines.

AFTER MEETING MEETINGS ARE A CURSE
These meetings drive me mad. They are ridiculous. We have just finished a meeting and then someone says, can I talk to you for a few minutes. They then go on to rehash everything that was just said, or they tell you everything that was wrong with how the meeting went on and how they have a better idea than everyone else, and so on. You get the picture. These meetings are wrong. The correct approach is to say, please call for another meeting so that we can all listen to your idea and leave it there.

They may have some genuine and valid points, but the reason you had a meeting in the first place was for everyone around the same table to discuss the subject, so why are you having a one on one after the meeting?

These type of meetings are the enemy of managing what you do with your time. You may get a reputation for being tough when you do not indulge in these kinds of conversations, but you will more importantly own your life.

WHAT'S LEFT ON YOUR LIST?
Nothing! Niiiiiiiiiice!

YOU ARE NOW THE MASTER OF YOUR TIME!

Well done. You have reached the point where you are the master of your time. You will know exactly what your day is going to be made up of from the first glance at your schedule. You can look at a whole week and know what is going to be going on in your week. You can see the empty spaces and decide what YOU WANT to do in those spaces. It is a wonderful luxury. Maybe you get to have lunch with someone, maybe you get to go home early one day, maybe you get to do some research about something that interests you.

DOES ALL THIS SOUND TOO PERFECT?
You tell me that you have a boss and your boss is unpredictable, and that your boss messes up your schedule with unpredictable calls and meeting. Ok. No problem. Remember all those little appointments for your tasks that you posted? They are not set in stone. You can just drag and drop them around. If you find that your boss needs to see you urgently then drag a few of your task appointments out of the way and make time. Why not? After all you are here to help your boss achieve his or her objectives.

Remember? Why would a boss need you if you are not going to be helping his or her efforts to build the business?

Meetings with the boss can be managed by you. Set up a time with your boss, ask for a meeting so that you can share three things with them.

1. What you got Done!
2. What you are doing (Done'ing!)
3. What you are going to do (get Done!)

What I reckon is that if every meeting between two managers were filled with these three things it would accelerate progress. Do it weekly and you are on the right path. I recommend that you instigate the meetings with your boss in a time of your suggesting and you will take greater control of your time.

THINGS I WANT TO LEARN OR REMEMBER
Sometimes I come across lessons that I really want to remember and that I want to make a part of my life. Here's what I do with those. I turn them into daily reminders until I achieve them. Let's say I want to reach a certain weight goal in my life. First I turn it into something positive. If I were to weigh a certain weight, then I would be fit and look good. I would feel healthy and powerful. Then I would think about how long it would take for me to get to that point where I feel fit and powerful. Then I set up a goal that I think I can reach. Let's say I want to lose 5kg in 10 weeks, which would be half a kg a week. So I break this down and then add a reminder in my daily calendar from now until the goal. Every day I am reminded that this goal is ON! I live towards my goal in my head and then I live it in my body.

If I want to remember something I make an appointment for it and put it in my calendar. That way I do not have to write it down somewhere on a list and try to remember where the list is. I will have a thought reminder pop up from time to time.

For example I was working hard on listening in meetings and reserving my opinion until the end of the meeting. So I created this thought "BE AIR". Air is all around us but never thought about. However we cannot live without it. I figured that this would be a great approach to a meeting. Be needed but not be the focus. So I went through my schedule and put a reminder before each meeting, "BE AIR". Oh what an impact that had on my meeting skills. Actually what I did as an added extra was that before meetings where I thought I may get emotional, I put an extra reminder into the middle of the meeting and set my phone on vibrate to remind me. It really worked. I became much more effective in meetings. Try it out.

NAGGING, WHINING, COMPLAINING & CRYING
Nagging is wrong. It simply means that you have failed and you are looking for someone to blame. Instead of nagging rethink what it is that you want to see happen, and then figure out how to make that happen, then go do it.

Whining is annoying. No one cares anyway. Just get over it already will you? Everyone else is busy too. They all have their own problems to solve and have no interest in yours. If you feel like whining just write it all down in an email to yourself and send it to you. Read it next day and see what you think about what you wrote!!!

If you are complaining it simply means that you have gotten separated from the cause. You were originally there to help make this organization reach a certain goal. Complaining was never part of the script. Complaining solves no purpose other than to draw attention to poor little you. Get up, get focused and get strong. Go out there and do good things for the business and within 24 hours you will already be feeling better.

Crying is reserved for those with emotional overload. It can happen. If it is going to happen get it over with. Let it all out. There is nothing wrong with getting overloaded once in a very long while. It is a cry for help, so when you are crying and people are offering you help, accept it. Your body and soul were crying out for support, so accept the help you get, graciously. Nothing more destructive than a crying person saying there is nothing wrong with them and that they don't need any help. Go cry outside far away and come back when you are good if that is the case. Otherwise, open up and let someone in to give help.

COURTESY
If you want to be efficient with your time and get the most out of it, take note of this: When you are polite you accelerate communication. When you are rough or impolite you break trust and slow everything down. I have tried both. Positive and kind and giving spirits are quick to move forward. Grumpy, angry spirits hurt everyone. If you need to shout, go outside, and shout at the sky. When you are done come back. Shouting destroys.

GOSSIP
Kill the gossip. Walk away from people who are gossiping. Gossip is when two or more are talking about a person who is not present, and therefore unable to present their point of view. Ignore people who gossip. Call them out. Get them to invite the object of their gossip to discuss the situation. Do whatever it takes to stop gossip and do not participate in it. If you find yourself in gossip excuse yourself. Gossip is a time eating destructive force. Never engage in talking negatively or destructively about a person who is not present.

THE BOTTOM LINE ON TIME
Give 8 to 10 hours of amazing work. Be productive and deliver a great result. Be a light. Create new to do lists, disperse the tasks into your schedule, get rid of the to do list and live freely.

STOP AT CLOSED DOORS
The number of times that a closed door meeting is interrupted are innumerable. The door was closed for a reason. Respect a closed door and reconsider your need to enter the room. You will be a cause of distraction and you will disrupt the flow of thinking going on inside the room.

BE ON TIME
What can I say? I think those three words are of prime importance. Respect the appointment you have made sufficiently to get there on time, and if for some reason you are going to be late, then have the courtesy to inform the participants to your appointment of your lateness. And be honest! Don't tell them five minutes if you are still 15

minutes away. It does not help and creates anxiety and frustration.

THE TIME THAT REMAINS ON YOUR SCHEDULE IS BEAUTIFUL TIME.

Use it to make the world a better place. Learn something new. Create a new idea. Do something fun.

Always be willing to change and learn and grow, and use the time that you have wisely.

11 MOTIVATION & DELEGATION

A wonderful book to read is "The One Minute Manager" by Ken Blanchard and Spencer Johnson. This book is in and of itself transformational. I first read it at the age of 26 and it has guided my thinking since then. One of the lovely things about the book is that it is a narrative, and then key thoughts are written in huge words on a single page. There were several thoughts that stuck in my mind from that time, and the best one was this:

PEOPLE WHO FEEL GOOD ABOUT THEMSELVES PRODUCE GOOD RESULTS

I have seen this statement work out in countless circumstances over the years. I have seen live situations where, with just a few questions, a person has changed their perspective, felt good about themselves, and reaped wonderful benefits. Stopping smoking, losing weight, financial freedom, ending arguments. So much impact but such a simple idea. When you feel good, you are powerful. You have an "I can do anything" attitude. Is this the core of motivation?

Money, food, shelter, clothing, all appear in discussions about motivation. I ask, "Is it important to motivate people?"

You see, if you treat people with contempt, or confuse them with conflicting requests, or bind them with multiple masters, you create all the circumstances for failure. And yet, so many businesses operate this way.

The thing I have found out about managers is that the majority of them focus on getting what *they* want sorted out first. They make themselves comfortable and create their personal security so that they protect themselves from threats. They build up self-support systems that protect them, and they create the illusion of indispensability. The problem is, this self-protecting leads to using the people around them as soldiers in a campaign to defend a territory or protect a castle. Managers go on empire building campaigns for their own ends. Where is the business in all of this process? What business?

The majority of middle management are trying to survive and they will do whatever it takes to ensure that they are going to make it.

The business becomes a playing board, the people become the playing pieces, and let the game begin.

This leads to failure. Slow or fast, it leads to destruction of the business. People will begin to focus on the hurts they have, the lack of trust, the obligations that they have, and they will lose the will to contribute from their hearts.

The turnaround is pretty straight forward, start by thinking about what motivates you:

Let's wrte down 2 things that motivate you
1
2

Now let's write down 2 things that demotivate you
1
2

Just by looking at these four different thoughts, we will automatically have an inner prompting on what we need to change now in our business. If these things motivate you, are you providing them for your team? And if these two simple things demotivate you, are you doing them to the people that work for you?

Motivation has been defined as the "process that initiates, guides and maintains outcome-oriented behaviors"

If it is a process, it means it is something that we can learn how to do. If we apply effort to a task with the expectation of a certain personal result, and get it, we will feel a sense of success. The greater the measure of success, the more powerful the feeling of achievement. Desiring that sense of achievement is motivation.

To make the process work we have to be clear about WHAT is expected of our people, WHY they should do it, HOW it is going to be done, WHEN it will be done, and the REWARD they will have when they achieve what has been asked.

This is super simple.

One of the things I have noticed when asking managers about their personal work history is that they will share stories of how they were involved in some great crisis and how they participated in resolving it. The WHAT was pure, it was the desire to get the difficult task done by a certain time (THE WHEN), the WHY was also clear, they must get it done or the pain of failure would be too great to bear, HOW they did it, and the REWARD was seeing happy customers or happy bosses.

THE WHAT
THE WHY
THE HOW
THE WHEN
THE REWARD

These people were imagining the glory of completing the task and you seeing them light up. They talk with animation and emotion about how they achieved what they had set out to do. All it takes is to convert the work of your business into these five things and you will be well on your way to motivating your people. You see, once you have experienced the reward, you can easily visualize experiencing it again. What is interesting is that in very few interviews with managers do any of them speak about money. The stories are about them engaging in doing something meaningful, big and challenging, and completing it on time; and not about how they got a payment in their hands for completing a task.

If we want to motivate our people we want to create the same environment where they know what they are going to get out of doing a task, and that it has value.

Around the motivational issue is believing in your people and encouraging them to get on with what you have asked of them.

I BELIEVE THAT I CAN DO IT, THEREFORE I CAN
Visualization is important in the workplace. When people believe that they can do a certain task, they will perform it differently from when they feel unsure. Uncertainty is a drain on their mind, and will cause slow performance. Having full trust that they can do the task, and knowing that they have full support no matter the outcome will instantly improve the outcome.

People will take action when they think that by doing this task they will get what *they* want.

The problem is that just thinking you can do something is not enough to be able to do it. A lot of motivation falls down on this point.

If you can just think it, you can do it. No!

There is a part missing out of this statement,

If you can think it, then you are prompted to do it, now let me get what I need to be able to get it done

You do not need effort alone. So many funny anecdotes are commonly trotted out, such as you worked so hard to climb the ladder, only to find it was leaning against the wrong wall. You do not need effort alone. You need skills and you must grow your ability. Simple things will show us that this is true. Let's say we want to grow our business revenue by

10%. We tell our team that this is the goal, and we send them out to do it. What will be the result? Probably disillusonment and frustration. Why? Because there is only a WHAT. There has to be a WHY, a WHEN, a REWARD and a HOW. If we provide ALL the ingredients we will get the result that we want because your people will know what was expected, and if they achieve the goal, they will know that they have done well, and will have gained a reward that reinforces that achievement.

Celebration is a large part of motivation. One of the things I have been learning is that in setting up my goals there is lots of thought required. I take a long time to develop a real goal, sometimes it takes a week or so to just create a goal. The goal has a WHAT and a WHY. I know WHAT I want to do and I know WHY I want to get it done, but somewhere the HOW, the WHEN and the REWARD are still not clear. I must create a REWARD of what I will do when I reach the goal for the goal to start to mean anything. And I must have a clear picture in my mind of WHEN I will get it finished. Just going after goals is fairly pointless if it is only to tick off something from a list.

I have travelled a lot for business and for fun. One day, I realized that all of the sights that I see when I get where I am going look exactly the same in real life as they do in pictures. The only difference is that later on in life I will be able to look at my pictures instead of someone else's pictures and say, I was there. The reward of going to a place alone became empty and I stopped travelling for personal sightseeing unless there was someone on hand to go with. The difference in going with someone else multiplied the experience beyond my imagination. There was someone to remember with. And when we talk about that time, we grow our memory of that moment in time. The reward of the visit was in the sharing of the memories with someone else.

What is the point of all this? If there is no reward, no celebration of what has been achieved, then the brain will connect this to the idea that since there is no reward, there is no point in doing the activity. Therefore, to give my goal value, no matter how grand the achievement, there must be a meaningful celebration.

GET STARTED

We said that it is a process that INITIATES. That means gets things started. So often I spend time with a company or a group of managers and they get all excited about what they are going to do and how they are going to do it. The problem is, they don't do it.

This is the hardest part of any process. If you want to get your team motivated, you have to get started. Do something.

You can't draw on the experience of having done something if it just remains an idea. Too many people sit there with their ideas rolling around in their heads, but they never write them down. Many times during meetings I force people to write things down. Frequently senior managers come to meetings without anything to write with, and nothing to write on. If they don't write anything, they will instantly forget what they need to do. Something else that surprises me is how many times people write notes during a meeting and then just leave the paper on the table when they leave! They have lots of great ideas, but few of them ever become an actual task.

The tasks that you start become the things that you have done. The things that you have done become your experience. Your experience becomes what will help you to grow and get better and stronger.

So START!

GUIDES & MAINTAINS
The Process initiates and guides. It gets us started and then keeps us on track. When we are going after our goals it is so easy to get sidetracked, distracted from what it is that we want to achieve. Having that clear WHAT, WHY and WHEN in mind at the beginning will help us to keep focused on the goal. The motivation itself gives us the energy, the fuel required to keep us going.

Think about building a campfire. We go out and find the material that we are going to burn. We find some big logs that we can put in the heart of the fire as the main thing that is going to burn and provide heat. We put small combustible material in the bottom of the fire so that we can light it easily, and then we put the dry wood onto the fire, light it and away you go. Somewhere along the line the fire starts to die down, we need to refuel it. We need to keep it going, we add more fuel. If we did not prepare any, we will have to go and find some, or the fire will go out.

Motivation is all about keeping the fire burning. Adding more fuel as it goes along.

What is the job of management in keeping people motivated? Praise, encouragement, sincerity, and rewards (real ones), delivering them on time.

OUTCOME ORIENTED

Basically this is the objective of all motivation, to get a desired outcome. There has been much written about goals and so I will not spend too much time on it here. The most important part of goals are these

1. They must be written down
2. They must be readily and regularly available and reviewed daily
3. They must have a what
4. They must have a why
5. They must have a when
6. They must have a reward/celebration

The final word in our definition of motivation is behaviors.

Behaviors are important.

If we do an activity once it is just an experience. We did it and we move on. If you want to know how to play the guitar it is very simple. You pick up a guitar, put your fingers on the strings in the right place and strum the strings and you will get a sound. The challenge is to be able to do that over and over again, putting your fingers in the right place each time you strum and getting the sounds in a sequence and at a pace that creates a melody.

How do we get that skill? We keep on practicing. We work at it over and over again. It is insufficient to know how to play a C Chord. It must be playable instantly, without thought, in the sequence of a song, upon demand. This requires a behavior. What is that behavior? Constant practice and constant improvement. Keep on strumming, keep on pressing and eventually you will be able to do it.

The idea that having played the C Chord once is sufficient to be able to play the guitar is absurd and every reasonable person knows that.

So what happens when we go to work? Why do we expect that a different set of laws will apply? Of course the same set of rules will continue to be in play. If you want to become good at a specific activity in the workplace, then you are going to have to develop a behavior that is going to deliver that result. Will it work the first time? No. Will it work over time? Yes.

You must develop lots of little behaviors over time that create the results that you want to see in your life. If you want to keep your body in good shape, you must work out a certain number of times per week. You cannot keep all your workouts to one day a month and hope that will work. That would be foolish. The same applies for business. You must work on you each day. Become a better version of you today than you were yesterday.

BLOCKS
There are lots of blocks that pop up and prevent people from staying on track and one of the biggest ones is managers. The job of a great manager is to ensure that he is not stopping his people from performing. He must deliver

a work environment free of obstacles, careful discipline, compliment filled and praise oriented, without gossip.

Here it is for you in summary:

It is a process - not by chance
It must be started
You must have rules
You must maintain it
Keep your mind constantly on the goal and have great rewards
Develop behavior that will sustain your goals and grow your life

PRAISE
Praise keeps people going. It is an unwritten reward for your people. The more you use it the better they become. Step forward and encourage people. Practice encouraging random people so that it becomes a part of your daily life. When you go to the parking attendant, praise them; the bagging guy at the supermarket, the checkout person where you are paying for something, the waiter in a restaurant. Keep on going. Praise these people every day until praising becomes a part of your life. Be generous with your words. It costs you nothing but brings great reward. The reward is that your entire life will be affected. You will begin to see positivity around you wherever you go and you will find that people are attracted to work with you. Curb your desire to criticize. Everyone can do that.
Thought: A bad word never helped anyone.

DELEGATION IS THE OTHER HALF OF MOTIVATION
Simply, delegation is to have someone else be me.

What does that mean? To be me?

When I want to delegate, basically I am going to be giving away some of my work to someone else, and that person is going to be doing it instead of me. So what kind of person do I want to entrust with being me?

I want to give away as much of my work as possible to others, however I don't want to give it up altogether. Giving up altogether, letting go if you will, is called abdication. It happens a lot. Ask a manager what progress has been made on a certain project and they will tell you that they have given it to someone else to do and they are not sure. This is a clear sign of abdication. So often managers are not sure how to delegate their tasks, so the idea is shared to them that they should get others to do a part of their job. They hand off the task and for them, the job has been delegated. That is not what we want to see happen.

The power of delegation is amazing. It is an opportunity to get others in your workplace engaged in doing what it is that you are doing. They will become an important and integral part of the process and subsequently will feel a greater sense of value in what they are doing in the business.

The greatest benefit of delegation is that you clear out of your own way the things that others can be doing, allowing yourself more quality time to do things that need your attention and which you are probably good at. The process of getting others engaged is the smartest way to get more stuff done in a shorter space of time.

You build trust.

The more trust that exists, the faster your business moves.

You grow other people

The more that others grow, the more they feel they are progressing. Progress creates success and success leads to happiness.

Delegation creates happiness in the workplace!

What is the downside to delegation?

There really isn't one. You see, your people are getting new skills, junior team members are engaging in more important work and are closer to the mission, and because they are participating they can give more important feedback directly to you about how things are going. You will have better ideas, and that of course always motivates.

Delegation comes with responsibilities.

You must allow people to do things differently from how you would do them. Let them find their own way.

You must build a reporting feedback process that guarantees that you are not going to reach a deadline without knowing how things are going long before that time comes.

AGREE
WHAT is going to be done?

WHY it is going to be done?
WHEN it is going to be finished?

The how is up to them, but you will be able to give direction.

You see, it is very close to motivation. Just add one more thing to it and you are going to be complete: REWARDS & CELEBRATION.

The things is, with delegation you are making a deal. There are two parties to the task. You cannot come with a big stick and state what you want to have done, that is not delegation, which is just giving orders. Here you must discuss and agree together the deadline and deliverables. You see, if you have an even and balanced conversation the deadlines and deliverables will be much more realistic and probably more likely to be achieved.

80% of deadlines are self-imposed. We create them to invent a positive stress on the team so that performance will improve. Because of this, we can always adjust and adapt our deadlines to fit to the people that are going to deliver them. Clients would far rather be delivered something of quality and value later than they had hoped, rather than rubbish that does not work in a shorter and unrealistic time frame. Keep this in mind.

Your job as the delegator is to explain WHAT is required from your point of view. The other party (or team) may have many more add ons and activities around the WHAT that you had never considered. Be ready to absorb those.

Be clear about WHY this job needs to be done by them. Give a lively WHY and you will inspire enthusiasm into your team.

For the WHEN, ask them first. Ask when they think they will be able to complete this assignment. They will surprise you. If you start off by saying I need this by Friday automatically that will fire something in their heads that they are being pushed. Ask the question of them, when do you think you could deliver this and the majority of reasonable team members will be pleased do surprise you and will come back with a delivery date that will exceed your expectations. What you do once a due date has been figured out is to set an interim review date with them where you are going to discuss the project and progress. This review date (or several if it is a big task) is going to be long enough before the delivery that you are going to be able to jump in and help out if things are falling behind.

Give responsibility and you will get nice surprise.
Give orders and you will get disappointments

WHAT SHOULD I DELEGATE?

This is a great question that many really struggle with. Here is how I work through this one. Keep an inventory of every single task that you do for a week. An entire week. Note down every single little thing, big or small. This will take some commitment on your part, but stick with it, because at the end you are going to have the opportunity to get rid of a lot of tasks that you really do not need to be doing.

At the end of the week you will be able to look through your tasks and put a note next to each one, by categorizing them like this:

A — Things I love to do and that light me up with passion
B — Things I am good at and that need my attention
C — Things that I am obliged to do because they need to be done

Your goal is to delegate everything in C. EVERYTHING. Figure out a way to delegate it, outsource it, and hire someone to do it and to stop doing it forever.

Once you have done that, and it will take you some time, you repeat the exercise of noting down everything you do on a daily basis again. Re-categorize all your work into A, B and C. You will find that tasks that were originally in your A list have slipped down into B, and tasks that were in your B list have now become your new C tasks.

So ther what do you do? You got it! You give away all your C tasks and repeat the exercise.

This is a powerful purification process. Over time you will end up solely doing valuable activities. Everything you do will be important and add massive value. Not only that, you will no longer waste your days. You will feel a sense of excitement and fulfillment in all that you do. Your people will be growing because you are constantly giving them more and more important things to do and they are growing too.

CREDIT WHERE CREDIT IS DUE
When you delegate it is no longer you who did the job. Remember that and give the praise and credit to those who actually did the job. Let them enjoy the joy of participating in this process.

FEAR
A lot of managers do not like to delegate. They are afraid. They are insecure about their positions so they figure, if they delegate they will not have anything important left to do and their team will become a threat. This is complete rubbish. Your team will feel a sense of loyalty and commitment like never before because you are leading them.

It may be faster if you do it yourself. The first time that is true. In the long term this is not true. You see, yes, there may be a mistake the first time that someone does one of your tasks, but hey, were you perfect the first time you did something? I doubt it. So get over yourself. Let it be done a bit slower than you can do it for a while and as they become experienced at doing the task, it will speed up and eventually you will never have to do that task again.

What if things happen that you do not know about? Well that's just life. You cannot know everything anyways! However, if you have delegated well and set up interim meetings between task start and end, you will have lots of feedback along the way so surprises will be few.

What if they don't do it your way? That's great. You may learn something too! The idea is to relax control, but to keep the standards. HOW is up to them. The goal of our work is to get the job done and make customers 100% happy. The goal is not to do it MY way.

As you delegate you become less of a specialist and more of a generalist. Sometimes this is tough, because we are letting others do work that we used to do and that we are good at doing. Our insecurity is going to appear in the things that we are now doing where we are learning. Because we have delegated tasks we are now going to be able to tackle new challenges and that means we are going to be entering a new phase of learning and the possibility of us making mistakes. Remember, that is the exact same way your people feel!

Let go and be the guide.

MR DOITALONE	MR DELEGATOR
Does it all himself	Delegates
Achieves good results	Achieves great results
Works long lonely hours under pressure	The team works with him

TEAM FEELING

| Watch him run around | participate/help out |
| Good friends with everyone | Friendly and respected |

OUTCOME

| MR DOITALONE | MR DELEGATOR |

Overworked
> Efficient

Team take a ride
> Team share the work

Limited personal growth/development
> Teaching/Learning/Growth

Stagnation and demotivation
> Flexible/helpful/enthusiasm

HERE'S WHAT TO DO:
1. Analyze your work for a week and make a list
2. Categorize your work in A (Passion work) B (Things I am good at) C (Obligations)
3. Assess team members' suitability for tasks from list C
4. Meet and set out the WHAT and WHY, agree on the WHEN & the REWARDS/CELEBRATION
5. Ensure that you have review dates and stay committed to them
6. Supply support as much as is required
7. Report back to your boss on what you have achieved!
8. Give praise generously

MY DECISION:
It is time to take some decisions. I suggest that you write them down right now while this is fresh in your head and hopefully you are inspired to do so.

I will start to monitor all my activities this week so that I can categorize my tasks and identify what I will delegate. I will do this by _____

I will motivate my _____ by
_____
_____
_____

I will delegate

WHAT   WHY   WHEN
                REWARD

12 EVALUATIONS REVISITED

Ready to change the way you think? By now, I hope you are.

Here we go. Take your old evaluation process and throw it away!

Hahahaha. I am sure that you are struggling with that concept. Everyone does. Actually I am just laughing like crazy as I write this. I can see your face. You think I am nuts. But hey, who cares, let's figure it out and you may change your mind. Let's see.

Performance reviews were first created quite a long time ago, and for many they are now sacred parts of their working life. After all, they do make a lot of people feel important. They keep the mass in control, they provide a bunch of complex tools to keep people in their place and control the payroll costs. They are actually quite a communistic tool in the wrong hands. I am sure you are not like that, right? But others have been known to use evaluations for wrong motives.

Back in the industrial revolution (which is actually so long ago that no one can even remember what that was all about), dear Adam Smith, who has been dubbed the Father of Capitalism, figured out that we should have simple tasks and specialized tasks and there became a division of labor. There were horrific conditions where children worked, long days were the norm and there were few safety rules. Wages were low. Unions began to appear and were created to campaign for the rights of workers.

As time progressed many parliamentary acts were passed and in the early 1900s the science of management began to appear, and along with it came measurement of employee performance. Studies were conducted that measured the productivity of workers in relation to their work environment, and then in the Great Depression in 1929 the government began to step in and dictate that there should be pensions, labor standards and minimum wages. By the 1940s there was a recognition of the social needs of employees and there was an understanding of the effect of good leaders and wise counsellors on the workforce. In the 1950s the US Government decided that there would be a 3 rating system of all employees that would be conducted to determine if an employee was unsatisfactory, satisfactory or outstanding. It was called the Incentive Awards Act. In the 1960s a further Act supported increases for performance, and so began this mess that we are now in. MBO (management by objective) became important in every company and everyone was measuring everyone else. But underlying all of this, don't forget it was not first set up for the improvement of the workforce, it was motivated by money.

By 1992 a national study in the US found that only 20% of the workforce were satisfied with their performance review. My guess is that the 20% that were happy with them are those who were at the top of the tree (but that is just a guess).
Just five years later in 1997 only 5% of people who were in a performance review process were satisfied. And yet companies continued to use them, and not only use them, but insist on doing them. Remember, only 5% were

satisfied, and yet 95% of the workforce were subjected to something that did not make them satisfied.

Then the whole process went online and became digitized. Employees began working remotely, and became more aware. It was determined that evaluations DESTROY morale, KILL teamwork and HURT the bottom line.

In 2009 Reuters reported that 80% of the workforce was DISSATISFIED with the entire process. 80% = MOST PEOPLE

> JUST BECAUSE YOU HAVE ALWAYS DONE PERFORMANCE REVIEWS FOR EMPLOYEES DOES NOT MEAN THAT YOU HAVE TO KEEP ON DOING THEM

Think about the amount of work that goes into them. Think about the value that comes out of them. Think about the dissatisfaction with the process. If employee evaluations were a social media they would have crashed and gone a long time ago.

So why do they still exist?

Einstein said something along the lines of "if we keep on doing the same thing the same way and expecting a different result, this is the definition of insanity".

If you do what you always did, you get what you always got.

The system is broken, so we need to fix it. We live in a new world of connectivity. Life today is different from just 5 years ago. Social media is shifting our workplaces and if you are in customer service you will have felt the weight of social impact on your business. A bad review of your service can truly harm you.

So it is with annual reviews. Why would you want to make 80% of your people unhappy because of an outdated process? Do you need an annual review that MOST of your people don't like?

I don't think you do. Annual reviews are ridiculous. You mean that once a year you are going to tell me how I am doing? And if you do biannual reviews, you are going to tell me twice a year what you think? This is not right. You have to be better than that. Things are changing by the week. There are new trends. Employee turnover is rising. If you are going to wait for an annual review the majority of your front line and junior team members are either going to have left for a new job or be doing something different from what they were doing one year before. Now tell me that an annual review makes sense.

Oh yes, our senior team should have annual reviews you say. No. Please. Your business is worth so much more than that. Your top team do not need an annual or biannual review. They need something much more timely. Something more engaging and that respects their intelligence.

The driving reason you have been doing these evaluations is simply because of one main key factor:

MONEY

The evaluation system was created for, and has been used to figure out when we will give people an increase, and when they will get more, and how much they will get.

Here's a revision of the whole system

FROM TODAY ONWARDS:
Evaluations will have just 2 questions.
What do we want to know?

QUESTION 1
Are you happy with your employees' results?
YES OR NO

If yes, tell me what you like and I will give you more

If no, tell me what you don't like and I will change.

QUESTION 2
What do you think about how I do it?
LIKE/DON'T LIKE

If you like it, tell me what you like and I will give you more of what you like
If you don't like it, tell me what you don't like and I will change it

YOU ARE DONE!
Evaluation is over.

Now let's flip it around and let them answer these questions:

QUESTION 1
Do you know what to do?

QUESTION 2
Do you know how to do it?

QUESTION 3
Do you do it?

QUESTION 4
How much can we trust you? (1 - 10)

ASK
What ideas do you have?
What things do we need to do or have to make work better?
What do you want to be in the future?

The only thing that is left is to tell them any important personal comments
I WOULD ALWAYS WANT THIS PERSON ON MY TEAM

I WOULD GIVE THIS PERSON THE HIGHEST COMPENSATION POSSIBLE

So what do we do about the MONEY?

Let's give this whole process a positive and happy meaning. No more corporate rubbish. Quit the blah blah blah and corporate nonsense.

BIRTHDAYS

These are days to celebrate and have fun. Everybody loves a birthday. So let's help our people really celebrate their birthday, celebrate life and celebrate their contribution.

There are three kinds of money that we are going to give our people.

INFLATION COMPENSATION
REWARDS
INCREASES

INFLATION COMPENSATION
Inflation compensation is the easiest of the three. We adjust everyone's salary by an arbitrary percentage every year in line with inflation. That would mean that prices on services and products would increase as would cost of labor, retaining parity. Announce it on January 1st each year and make the adjustments accordingly. On the birthday of your employee you give them the percentage for inflation compensation directly in their salary. What this means essentially is that you have spread the percentage increase over the entire year. You will be able to calculate the increases as an exact science in your company due to the fact that you have all the data of every employee.

REWARDS
The reason that an employee deserves more money is quite simple really. This person has contributed a year of their life to your organization. They have given you their talents and efforts and they have continued to do so. What if we gave each employee a reward? The longer they stay with you, the greater the reward. So instead of trying to

measure someone's commitment in a very subjective manner, how about we do it objectively and give to people who stay with us? Each employee gets to pick out a reward of choice. We create a basket of different rewards for the different lengths of time served.

Now what is interesting about this is that we can calculate a budget for this activity with accuracy, and we can adjust it in times of difficulty or in times of plenty. Gifts can expand or decrease according to the general business climate. There are other benefits about the gift system. The gift is separate from the payroll. It is a gift. Therefore it does not increase the base pay of an employee. This is so helpful in keeping line employee with tenure salaries in place. It means that a line employee with 5 years of service would not have a basic salary that has gone over the end of some scale or another. The line team member will be drawing a gift from the gift box.

How does the gift box work? HR can calculate exactly how many employees there are in each year of service in the company quite simply by entering the employee start date into the computer. That will give a report of how many folk there are in each year. Then you gear up the gifts based upon the total increase that the company can afford to give within the year and still maintain the costs and profits ratio. So for example if the entire budget for increases other than inflation is 5% of turnover that will give a budget that can be quickly calculated.

If you provide inflation at 2% and then say 7% growth on salaries, then you have a number to work with. Take the total payroll and divide it up by number of years served, then calculate the gift that you would give them from our tool www.done.fyi here. What this does is it allows you to give an increase without accumulating it onto the payroll. So if you give a gift of $420 to someone whose increase would be a cumulative $420 for the year, then you are doing something great for them. They will receive their total annual increase, which is just $45 a month, in a onetime lump sum. Now here's where it gets more interesting, the longer you stay the more it appears to be. Someone that has 10 years of tenure is going to be getting a gift of $1055 in their pocket. This simulation is given for someone who is earning $500 per month, and their ten year salary is compounded to provide the equivalent.

In all cases this works out more cost efficient for companies. If the gifts are really attractive, then this shifts the focus from cash to other things. For example you may have a gift voucher for $500 for a store in the city, or you may choose to have $410 in cash, which would you go for? Now when you go to the store in the city and tell them that you want to buy $10,000 of vouchers discounted by 20% you can bet that they are going to say yes. Now you are leveraging your cash. You can get your team to say what kinds of gifts they want to have. Tickets for flights, for special events, all kinds of things can be created to be put into the box.

How does it work? On a birthday you go to your HR website and select your gift, click and HR will add that gift to you. Simple!

What a great birthday!

INCREASES

Increases are the third kind of money. What are these? Well it is quite simple, when someone deserves to get a raise, they get one. Leaders know when they have a team member that is suitable for another position. There are salaries assigned to positions. Promote the person when they are ready and pay them accordingly.

This makes the company very fair.

Think -
How can I help my people to grow?
How can I help my people help my people to grow?
How can I engage the group to power my business?

But hang on you say. What about all those important questions we used to ask employees during evaluations? What happens to those? They were important. What will we do now?

My answer is, "What were those questions really all about?" The questions that asked about team cooperation, commitment to company goals, dedication to the life of the company.

Forget them!

Make working in a company all about living a better life. Make it about getting a dream car, going on an amazing vacation, having great medical insurance, children's education funded, credit card debt paid off.

What if working for your company was all about investing time and effort because it would result in worthwhile rewards and not just a standard few dollars of increase?

What if you truly felt that you have the opportunity to do your best every day, and that it would be recognized?

What if managers were no longer holding the scales of justice over you and preparing to pronounce judgment on your contribution once or twice a year?

Evaluations were a system driven by fear and punishment with illusionary rewards.

Was anyone truly inspired by fear? Probably motivated to run away, seek a different place to work, but not to contribute their best.

PERFORMANCE

Performance must be evaluated you say. I AGREE.
You should be talking about employee performance all the time. Every day, every week. At meetings, during a coffee. You have INSTANT CONVERSATIONS.

A talk about performance is not to be put off for a second. It is not to be held back for a special day in a few months from now. That is cowardly. Talk to your people now. Keep notes. Help them to get better. Set up some exciting goals that will get them contributing to the business and encourage them to produce outstanding results.

What about measurement of employees? What about all the numbers we used to produce? The graphs that used to show the best, the mass and the worst? What about the bottom 10% that we are supposed to chuck out? They are no longer here in our companies! We dumped them.

Are you going to have a long conversation with me on this? I hope so, but I suspect that you are not going to be bringing in new ideas. The system is broken. Don't bring something broken and say it's good enough. Remember 80% of people are dissatisfied with evaluations.

Administrators love the evaluation process. It gives them a freaky sense of control and puts them in a place of power. What a load of nonsense. Since when has all that had a positive impact on customer service? How does that help us do a better job of being a great business?

But what about goals? We have to have goals, right? Right! However the whole point of having goals is to ensure that work is progressing forward towards things of value to the business. Not for the sake of having goals. And not for further lining the pockets of executives who are already well paid. Goals are a way to get things on track and keep it going the right way. They were not invented that you get a larger slice of the pie.

What about financial KPIs? Bonuses?

SERIOUSLY????

If you implement the system of Inflation compensation on employee birthdays, you provide them with clear rewards, and you give raises on time, do you think that people deserve even more after all of that? You should rethink your thoughts on work and what it is that someone is hired for.

The objective is that you go to work and add value to the business by using your talents as best as you can to make this company succeed as much as you can. In return you get a fair part of the proceeds of the business. The higher the value you add to the company, the greater the share you are entitled to receive.

A good business will always truly take care of its employees. It will help employees satisfy their needs while meeting the needs of the business.

A good business will help employees understand that it cares for them.

A good business will help employees understand that it listens to them.

A good business will help employees understand that it values their ideas

A good business will help employees solve the small issues that drive them nuts

A good business will help employees get formal papers done for banks and so on

A good business will help employees get what they need when they are in need

A good business will help employees by being a center for problem solving for their lives

WHY?
Doing good for employees is doing good for our business. Taking care of those inside our business is our greatest CSR activity ever. Before giving to others or spending valuable dollars on marketing or advertising, we make sure that we have the happiest, best cared for team in the world.

No to disengaged employees
No to dissatisfied employees

YES to feeling good.
YES to being a part of it
YES to sharing the rewards for their hard work
YES to every single person in our company living a fulfilled life
YES to being truly employee centric

Let's evaluate shall we?

This all sounds too good to be true right?
Let's evaluate.
Let's be better.
Let's be better than we have ever been.
Actually, let us be the very best we can be
Or, perhaps, just, The Best!

13 INTERVIEWS - THE FIRST 10 SECONDS

In the matter of hiring people I have a simple philosophy.

HIRE THE RIGHT PEOPLE
HIRE BRIGHT PEOPLE

Lots of employees say they are bored with their jobs. Wherever I go around the world I hear that same message. They are bored with the day to day humdrum business that they are required to do. No change, just an ongoing average expectation of producing more of the same without rocking the boat.

I want amazing employees in my organization and I imagine that you do too. You have probably hired a lot of people and read a lot about interviews. Here's my take on hiring great people.

1 FORGET NORMALITY
Before the interview is about them it is about you. What is your story? Are you happy?
How can you be interviewing someone to join you if you are not into this work? This is the bedrock of what to expect in the future. A simple job in the company must have the same level of passion injected into it as a complex one. We need every person that joins us to be a part of our tribe. A believer in what we do.

2. IMAGES ARE POWERFUL
Pictures tell stories. Figure out who you are. Get a picture that shows who you are.

Right now, go search online for a picture that shows us who you are. Post it somewhere with the caption, ME.

Now that you have your image let's get you a story. Describe your life in six words. There are lots of ways to do that.

LEARN - UNDERSTAND - REFORMULATE - SHARE - NURTURE - REPEAT
BRAINWASHED - PUZZLED - CONFUSED - AWAKE - AWARE - ALIVE
PLAY SAFE - MISS LOTS OF STUFF
GO OUT AND TAKE FRIGHTENING RISKS
YOU CAN DO WHATEVER YOU WANT

MY 6 WORD STORY: (Yep, go ahead and write it - share it with me if you don't mind)

_____ _____ _____
_____ _____ _____

We need a fresh start. We have to look at interviewing candidates from an entirely new and different perspective. First we get ourselves ready.

Know your story. Have your picture. Now you are ready! Ready for what?

The best conversation of your life. Pour yourself into it. You never know, perhaps you are interviewing your life partner

10 SECONDS
In the first ten seconds that you spend with this person I want you to think,

How does this person make me feel?
Are they happy?
Do they look good?
Do they have a positive greeting?

However this person makes me feel is pretty much the impact that they are going to have on my customers and on my other team members. For the way they are on interview day is who they are when they are putting their best face on.

Are they happy? You can't make sad people happy. That just never works. If they have an unhappy disposition on interview day, they are unlikely to change for the better. Most people consider an interview an opportunity to make a good impression and to show their best side. If they are not going to make me feel happy, is this a person I really want to have in my team?

It is not about being nervous. Nerves are fine. Making me feel happy will shine through their nerves.

Looking good is important. I don't mean that they are wearing a suit by Prada or something silly like that. I mean that they have done the job of washing and brushing themselves up. Way back when, in the 1980s you had to wear a suit and a tie. In this generation just about anything goes in clothing and piercings and tattoos. All of that stuff is part of the way life is today. But that does not mean that they cannot look good. A beard? Groomed. Long hair? Clean. Hands and nails well taken care of. Those are the signs of looking good. Smell good. Clean but not overwhelming. If they look good it means that they have taken the time to do so. That's a good thing. We want to have people in our team that look good.

The greeting has to be positive. A good handshake. A warm smile. Positive.
You only get a split second to make a first impression. Let it be awesome. Does this person have a positive greeting? Do I feel that I am in the presence of goodness? Our business is all about instant connections, any customer service business is. So we must ensure that every single greeting is valuable and communicates goodness.

HELP!
Help the candidate to feel good. Do your part. Welcome them by name.

Introduce yourself properly. Make your own name clear.

I always say, welcome, my name is Mark. I am going to be meeting with you today.
Then I ask a simple question related to getting here. And then I wait. I don't talk.

Let them talk. Listen and nod your head.

Then ask them what they are here for. Make sure that the job title s clear.

Look for character. Not just anyone. Look for someone that stands out from the others.

QUESTIONS I ASK
   a. Tell me where you last worked and what you liked about your last job
   b. Who was the person you most liked working with
   c. Who was the worst person you worked with
   d. Why did you leave/are you leaving?
   e. When have you been so busy that you lost track of time? What were you doing?

Ask them to tell you about their career. Tell them you read their CV but you would like them to walk you through the journey. Remember to ask why they would like to work here, and ask them about their future dream. Try to figure out how long you think they would be ready to work for your company, normally I am very direct and say, "What sort of time-frame are you putting on this job? A year? Two years?" and I do it in a casual conversational sort of way. Their answer will immediately tell me if they fit what I have in mind. A senior who is looking for a one-to-two-year position is possibly not the fit I am looking for.

Ask them what they would feel if they didn't get this job. How they answer this question will give you a sure indication of their job search and their desire to work with you.

When I am done with these questions, I am pretty much done with them. So I ask them what questions they have. Simple: "What would you like to ask me?"

When it comes to compensation they will often ask about the package. I like to turn it around and say, "What is your expectation?" Typically candidates will hesitate. What I will learn from this question is the value that they put on themselves. Some are silly and ask way too much for the job. I ask them why they put that value and then listen. Ego will often come into play and they will put their cards on the table about their value. If they put it too low it means that they are desperate to get a job, not necessarily this job. If they prevaricate it means that they do not yet have a grasp of their own value.

TEST YOURSELF
This is a mental exercise that I play with myself. I visualize myself introducing this person to others, often I try to actually get other members of my team to pop in and say hi during the interview. I observe how they react to the other team members and observe their greeting with people who the candidate will not perceive as part of the interviewing process. This is a great indicator of how they will interact with people that they are unprepared to meet.

Here's what I ask myself:

Can this person do the job?
Is this someone I would like to introduce to the rest of my team?
Would I be proud to introduce them to the team?
Would they fit in and help us become better?
Would they be able to take over in five years from now (or less)?

If you have created an opportunity for this person to meet with other team members listen to what the team have to say about them.

Don't be afraid to take a picture of them. I even take videos of some of my candidates. I tell them that we do loads of videos for our training and I think they would be a great person to be in our training videos and I would like to run a quick test.

The results are awesome. I do it with my phone, get them ready and ask, "Why would you like to work here?" People start to gush forward with their enthusiasm and you catch it all on cam. Really fun. Revolutionary. And it will help you in the decision process. You can also share the video with people in your team whose opinion you appreciate.

WHAT DOES SUCCESS TODAY MEAN?
Let them know what comes next. Talk about the money and prepare them for what will happen from here on.

BE NICE
If today is a no, it does not mean I have to be negative. Think positive. It has happened before where the interviewer later on in life becomes the interviewee. If you were nice you will leave a good impression that will only have a positive effect in the future. Smile a lot.

Something else that is important to remember: This person is a customer.

Say a nice goodbye.

14 THE WAY WE TALK

There is a lot to be said about the way that managers work, walk and talk. There is massive accountability on our shoulders from the day that we are appointed as a manager. It's important. It's big. It's not small.

SPEAK WHEN IT IS YOUR TURN
Always have something useful to say.
I was in a company this morning for a meeting about the future direction of the company. This operation has several hundred employees and the meeting included the top level of managers. We asked the owners to share their vision for the future of the business, and as one would expect, they shared deeply from the heart, exposing their passion and joy and love for what they do, and their enthusiasm to grow the business bigger and to go further and do more.

Having listened to everything they said we then asked the managers to share their vision. What a sad testimony to the maturity of the company. The managers had a few strangled words to contribute. What does this mean? Are they bad managers? No. They just do not understand the importance of what it means to be a manager. This was their moment to shine. To show what they have bottled up inside and to bring it into the light.

If you go off to the coffee room later on you will most likely hear some kind of grumbling related to the experience. Managers are duty bound to be ready to contribute intelligently when it is required. To participate at the big table and share the dream and love for the business that they have been entrusted with.

DON'T SPEAK WHEN IT IS NOT YOUR TURN
Equally, learn to shut up.
The less words you say when it is not your turn to speak, the better it will go with you. Arguments and fights cannot be won, so don't waste time in getting into one.
You see, if you think that you won a fight, then it means that someone else lost. If you are aware of the world that we live in today, most people who lose, take up their cause and seek justice, they gather others around them to support their point of view and will become a center of negative energy. See to it that no one loses.

Find the way to ensure that everyone will win.

Remember there is a triple win. There is the win-win of those who are in the room, and there is a third win that is related to those who are not present. Make sure that on every occasion everyone wins.

DON'T GET CAUGHT OUT
If you speak out of turn, if you say something mean, or criticize, there will be someone that is going to share what you said. The problem is that they will not share it the way that you said it. Remember, everything you say can and may be used in evidence against you. The less bad things you say, the better your life.

Avoid getting caught up in the moment.
Sometimes when things start to heat up, emotions start to run, or people challenge what you have said, it is quite easy to diffuse by backing down and apologizing. Sorry, I think I may not have expressed myself properly. Let me try again. Then rephrase what you want to say in a low key way.

Remember, a year from now, most of the meetings you have today will no longer be important. They will have faded out of memory. Being patient and holding back on feelings will give you many options for the future. Blasting it out right now will mean that you have no control over your words. You can always take a pause. Suggest that you can meet again on this so that you prepare yourself better.

Figure out ways to talk to people about their performance and not about who they are as a person.

Gossip is the killer. Last week we had a meeting with a restaurant owner for two hours. All he talked about was other restaurant owners and how they were doing. When the restaurant owner asked me how other folks were doing, I said I didn't know. Why did I say that? Because I knew that I was going to be repeated, word for word for anything that I said. He had repeated to me what others had said, so he that is obviously his pattern, so he will repeat what I have said, and probably not in context! Do not talk negatively about anyone who is not present. It will always come back to you in the wrong way and at a time that is going to cause you the most discomfort.

Anyone who talks to you about someone is going to talk to someone about you

RESPECT IS THE BEST WAY
I lost some serious sleep for not handling an employee well. I bow my head in shame and say that I was taken to court and lost a case for being disrespectful. Would I do it now? No way! I learned something that I already knew, but at a very high price.

Always talk in a way that would make you proud if your words were to appear on CNN.

15 THE DETAILS ARE IN THE SUGAR

Pareto's principle is based upon the discovery that 80% of income in Italy was earned by just 20% of the population. This principle has been extended to many areas of life, and frequently it stated that 80% of profits come from just 20% of customers.

Would it be fair to say that 80% of results came from just 20% of team members? Perhaps, if we separate the functions of thinking and doing.

Woody Allen said that 80% of success is just showing up. That is the 80 that I am interested in. So many people have read this far through the texts of this book and thought about a whole number of things that they should work on in their lives. The underlying theme to all of these pages is that of CHANGE. Personal change and process change.

Did you CHANGE from the time when you picked up this book and when you reached this page? I mean really change?

Did you decide to do something meaningful in your life that is just a ittle bit different from how you used to do things?

REALLY CHANGE?

Are you doing stuff differently?
Think about it for a moment...
We talked about:
           The art of thinking - flow-click-think

Change - focus-get help-remove inner conflicts

Influence - how to get what YOU want

Truly focusing on what you want and creating personal goals

Looking at numbers in business differently

How to sell using simple powerful techniques

How to evaluate your business using Sit & Watch

Managing how you use your time and eliminating to do lists

Motivating our people and delegating tasks to them

A new look on evaluating our team members

Rethinking our interviewing techniques

The way we talk as managers

Quite a journey. It began with a look at you as a person and then you as a manager.

What did you decide to change? Why not take a minute to write down one thing?

_____
_____

SHIFT YOUR PARADIGM

I was walking along the street a few weeks ago and there was a man leaning against the corner of our office building looking at the cars as they came in and out of the parking lot. I thought that he looked a bit unusual, I thought maybe he was looking at the cars to see which one he would take as his next target.

As I passed through the lot and collected my car, I dismissed the idea and went on my way. However, the next day as came into work I noted that the man was standing there again, looking pretty much the same as the day before, and still looking at the cars.

At first I noticed the man and always meant to drop a call to the local police, but as the days passed, never quite got round to it. Eventually, it became so normal to see the man standing there that I began to nod my head to him whenever we made eye contact, and he would nod his head in return.

One day I arrived at work a little earlier than usual and with time to spare, so I stopped the car, dropped the window and smi ed and talked to the man. "Hi, how are you?" he sort of grunted and nodded his head a bit. I ventured, "I see you here a lot, is everything ok?" and the man looked at me again, this time with more interest. "Yeah. I'm cool. Thanks". I responded with something like, "ah, ok" and decided to get on with my day and park my car. Why in the world would he be here every day? He seemed harmless enough. Somehow I felt good that I had said hello to him. My phone rang and I got wrapped up in the call and and forgot about the guy.

I was never to see the man again. Just one day later I see a picture on the local news about a man who jumped out onto the street to save a kid from being knocked down by a car. He saved the kid, but he died of injuries on the way to hospital. And the man who saved the kid? There he was, car park man; it was the same man who had stood at the parking lot each day.

A worthless man standing on the street?
A man willing to make the ultimate sacrifice for someone he had never known?

Who would have thought it? I felt different.

THIS IS CHANGE

What is it going to take for you to change?

Something that is so startling that it makes you see everything differently from that moment onwards. Kind of like when you almost crash your car, but you don't. Or when a plane is landing and it starts to slide on the runway and for a second you think, "This is it", but then it isn't and that moment makes you change just a little bit.
There are plenty of clichés out there about change. Beyond all the things that need to change, the most important is getting started. Take a step.

READ YOUR LETTER
The letter that you wrote at the beginning of reading this book is now ready for reading, (unless you read the whole book in one sitting - in which case, mail the letter to you for about 21 days from now), you will see that there are changes that you wrote about it in your letter that have already begun to happen in you.

That's because you made the conscious decision to entrust to your mind the power of change. Set something in motion that cannot be stopped. Make a difference to this industry, to your workplace. Be better than you have ever been before.

The Details are in the Sugar
What does this mean?

Sugar tastes good and all that, and it can definitely lift our spirits, but for me, sugar tells me everything that I need to know about an operation, a food and beverage business. If you want to know how things are going, then just look in the sugar bowl.
There are so many variants. Is the sugar in packets? Are the packets aligned? Are the logos all the same way? Is the white separated from the brown? Are they organized? Is there sweetener? Is there an equal quantity of white and brown? If you remove the sugar from the container, is the container clean underneath? Is the outside of the container clean?

Is it loose sugar? Then is it clean? Pure and white? Is the bowl clean inside and outside? Is there an under liner plate? Is that clean? Are there any chips or cracks in the sugar bowl?

Is the bowl made of metal? Is the metal polished? Is it shiny? Is there a paper liner under the sugar bowl to stop it sliding around on an under liner plate? Is it clean?

So many questions.

NOW I KNOW EVERYTHING!

Excellence in hospitality is in the details. It is all about making sure that the tiny things are in place. Big things are big. They are easy to see and easy to fix. You can take broad actions and get the results that you need. But the small things are small. They are the things that make the difference.

Managers, you, must focus on the tiniest details. Not a popular thought with most employees. They don't want to be bothered to go that far.

So why Sugar?
Because this is literally the smallest detail in service.

What does it take to get the sugar right? It takes outright passion. Flat out dedication and commitment.

It means that you will be addicted to the never ending process of doing things better and better. Getting into the tiniest of details because you know that this is where the difference will be made.

If every employee is engaged in a culture where the tiniest details count, then there will be a transformation in the way that training is being done. There will be a change in the way that team members will interact with each other.

There will be a TIRELESS commitment to excellence. It will be based on a PERSONAL COMMITMENT.

Many think that excellence is a place to go to. It is not. Excellence is a journey. As far as you can go today, you can still go further tomorrow. You can go one more step.

It is not about being good.

It is not enough to be better.

It is only done when it is BEST.

What is best? The best in the world?

NO

When it is the very best that you can produce. When you have expended every single bit of energy you have to get it where you think it can go, and then you figure out that you can take it still further. That is when it is BEST.

80% is easy.

Most companies can do it. They can get 80% of the way to where they need to go. Why? Because that is the big stuff.

90% is where it gets hard. Challenges really start to push back. Being at 90% is right out there on the edge.

95% is really cranking it to the limits.

But none of these are the goal.

100%

That's where the goal is at!

100% happy customers
100% of the time.

That and nothing else.

It is only attainable by observing the details.

By questioning everything

Constant listening

If things don't feel right, it means that they are probably not. So sit quietly and start to ask questions. Search. Determine that you will figure out why this is not working as it should, and then make it do so.

100% comes from the decision to NEVER COMPROMISE. I mean that you cannot compromise. Don't look around and start telling people not to compromise. That is not acceptable. No way. You must be truly focused on doing whatever it takes to take things all the way to the very end. Put every effort to make things excellent.

Tell your people stories.

BE THE EXAMPLE

Addicted to sugar? Need to get rid of your addiction?

Don't!

Stay addicted to sugar, but the right sugar!

16 THANK YOU

It has been a long time dream of mine to reach this part of my book. The book has long been in my head and in my heart. It is a letter of love to every manager in the hospitality industry. Thank you for reading. I know that if you will explore the way you do stuff, and if you will go after your personal decisions, you will change.

You will change you.

You will change your people.

You will create change in this world.

Your happiness will grow, your energy levels will be higher, your performance will have improved, and you are already a better person.

And I am a better person for knowing that you read this far.

GIVE - LOVE - SERVE

Book me to deliver this course to your management team

My company is called Done! and you can find us on www.dcne.fyi

We provide this book as a training course called Management Development Program. We deliver it live in 12 sessions of 3 hours each. We deliver it in three full days, or over a number of weeks, depending upon the organization. We have delivered it in Cambodia, Hong Kong, Bangkok, Japan, Dubai, Kuwait, Beirut and many other places. We are just a flight away. Get in touch with us on mdp@done.fyi and we will be delighted to get in touch with you and to serve you and your team. We provide the whole course online with instruction videos for each chapter and the material is available for participants to keep and to share with others. You can subscribe for the online learning experience at www.done.fyi/mdp

Thank you!

MY NOTES
Write your thoughts down here...

MY PAGE FOR TEARING OUT AND CRUSHING INTO A BALL

www.ingramcontent.com/pod-product-compliance
Lightning Source LLC
Chambersburg PA
CBHW020642220526
45464CB00001B/257